Aokigahara

The Truth Behind Japan's Suicide Forest

Tara A. Devlin

Aokigahara: The Truth Behind Japan's Suicide Forest
First Edition: September 2019
Cover by: Emiru the Yurei
http://www.instagram.com/emiru_1860/

taraadevlin.com
© 2019 Tara A. Devlin

DISCLAIMER

This book features discussion of suicide which may be upsetting to some readers. If you or anyone you know would like to talk to someone, please don't hesitate to reach out for help. Visit https://www.iasp.info/ to find contact information your country, or call your local emergency number.

CONTENTS

INTRODUCTION

"THERE'S A DEAD BODY BURIED beneath that tree."

A short story by Japanese author Kajii Motojiro begins this way, although the tree in question is a cherry blossom, one of the most popular symbols of death and rebirth in Japanese culture. The cherry blossom only blooms for a brief period during the spring, and then the flowers wither away, fading from sight until the following year. Thanks to the popularity of Kajii's short story, there's a saying that cherry blossoms with deep red flowers have a corpse buried beneath them, which is where they get their colour. While the story is fiction and the cherry blossom legend just a myth, there *is* a place where bodies are buried beneath the trees; Aokigahara Jukai, or the Sea of Trees, on the northwest face of Mount Fuji.

Aokigahara is perhaps best known worldwide as the "Suicide Forest," but it wasn't always this way. From its explosive beginnings when Mount Fuji erupted over 1000 years ago, to its current reputation as a suicide spot, Aokigahara has seen and been through many things. What we now know as Aokigahara first began to take form towards the end of the Sengoku era, or the Warring States period. Despite the seeming impossibility of an entire forest taking root on a hard lava floor, the trees of Aokigahara conquered the odds and flourished, creating the eponymous "sea of trees" as it appears from above.

Over the years, Aokigahara and numerous locations within it have been worshipped. You can find numerous shrines and caves within the forest today that were once important religious sites, and people continue to make the pilgrimage even now. Mount Fuji itself is considered to be one of the most sacred sites in all of Japan, so it's no surprise that Aokigahara, the forest that beat all the odds, would inspire the same faith. Yet its density, its treacherous hardened lava floor, the twisting roots and slippery moss that covers everything make it a true force to be reckoned with.

It was in the 1960s and 70s that views of the forest began to change. A character from a popular novel travelled to Aokigahara to commit suicide, and it wasn't long until real life started to imitate art. As more people visited Aokigahara, its fame grew, creating a vicious cycle where the forest became known less as a sacred religious site and more as a popular suicide spot. Now, there are literally bodies buried beneath the trees. As the forest shifts and grows, those bodies that aren't discovered eventually find trees growing up around them. It's not uncommon to find skeletal remains entwined with the roots of the trees, returning to the earth as new life grows around them.

In this book, we're going to be looking at the history of Aokigahara; how it came to be, how it's different to other forests, and its long and colourful history. We're also going to explore how it came to be known as the suicide forest, why people continue to go there, the government's struggle with preventing suicides, and how the local police deal with the grim reality of discovering corpses with alarming frequency. We'll also be debunking some of the myths and legends that have grown up around the forest, as well as exploring some of the more interesting features you can find inside; both man-made and otherwise.

Aokigahara is a mystery, even to those who have dedicated their lives studying it. With this book, however, I hope it will become a little less mysterious, and you'll come to see why Aokigahara isn't just a "suicide forest," but an important part of Japan's cultural history. A beautiful, fascinating ecosystem that thrives against all odds at the base of Japan's largest and most important mountain.

Let's enter Aokigahara, the infamous Sea of Trees.

WHAT IS AOKIGAHARA?

LOOKING DOWN FROM MOUNT FUJI, a mass of dense forest spreads out so far and wide that it's like looking down upon an ocean of trees. Officially known as Aokigahara, the forest also goes by another name: Aokigahara Jukai, the Sea of Trees. Located on the northwest face of Mount Fuji in Yamanashi Prefecture, the forest covers roughly 25 to 40 square kilometres of land, depending on who you talk to. Aokigahara has no defined limits, so it's difficult to say exactly how big it is and where it starts or ends. It sits at an elevation of 900 to 1,100 metres above sea level, meaning temperatures drop well below freezing during the cold winter months. It is also perhaps well known for one other reason: it's one of the most popular suicide spots in the world.

1. EXPLOSIVE BEGINNINGS

IN JUNE 864, Mount Fuji erupted. This may conjure up images of smoke and lava billowing from the crater atop the massive 3,776 metre high mountain, but that's not really what happened. In fact, Mount Fuji has never erupted from its peak; every single eruption over the course of its history has taken place on the slopes.

Mount Fuji sits at the junction of three plates; the Eurasian plate, the North American Plate, and the Philippine Sea Plate. In addition, the Pacific Plate pushes underneath all three, resulting in Mount Fuji's volcanic activity. It's said that Fuji's main magma line runs from the northwest to the southeast. This line is where the eruptions take place, where the earth's crust is at its thinnest.

Let's go all the way back to the beginning. Mount Fuji began life roughly 700,000 years ago as Sen-komitake. The "sen" in this case means former. Sen-komitake was much smaller than the mountain we know now, but it erupted often and basalt continued to pile until it formed a new mountain known as Komitake around 200,000 years ago. This volcano remained active and roughly 100,000 years ago, the constant eruptions formed yet another mountain on top of the old ones, this time known as Old Fuji. Further eruptions continued, and around 10,000 years ago yet another new mountain was formed on top of the old, this time known as New Fuji, or the mountain we know today. Mount Fuji is actually several mountains built on top of each other like bricks, and this creates numerous spots on the slopes where the crust is much thinner than in other locations. When volcanic activity starts kicking up inside the mountain, these are the first areas to blow.

The eruption that created Aokigahara Forest is known as the Great Eruption of Jougan. The Jougan era lasted from 859 to 877, with the first eruption on Mount Fuji taking place in June 864. This wasn't the first time New Fuji had ever erupted, but it was the first time in modern history that an eruption of this scale had ever taken place. No doubt the villagers who lived in and around the area feared the mountain's rumblings, but they had no idea what was about to occur.

A large-scale fissure on the northwest side of the mountain erupted roughly 10 kilometres from the summit. This created what is now known as Mount Nagao, a parasitic cone on the northwest slope of Mount Fuji, that spewed forth over one billion tons of volcanic debris. Over a period of two years, numerous craters and fissures opened on Fuji's northwest side, raining fire down upon the countryside. The *Sandai Jitsuroku*, a Japanese history text completed in 901—less than forty years after the eruption—mentions that there were three earthquakes before Fuji exploded, and then flames shot 60 to 70 metres in the air. Literal curtains of fire roared out of the mountain, pouring down its side and destroying everything in their path. The lava measured over 1,000 degrees Celsius. Nothing could withstand it. The people, the animals, and of course, the forests that had once grown there all died.

At the bottom of Mount Fuji lay a rather large lake known as Senoumi. It's mentioned in the *Sandai Jitsuroku* that the provincial governor of Suruga Province (present-day Shizuoka) informed the Royal Court that the lava had reached Lake Motosu, a lake at the bottom of Mount Fuji, located to the right and slightly forward of Senoumi. The provincial governor of Kai (present-day Yamanashi), on the other hand, informed the Royal Court that not only had the lava reached Lake Motosu, but that it had filled in Senoumi, splitting it in two. The lava kept going, according to the governor, all the way up to Lake Kawaguchi, a lake further northeast of Senoumi.

According to the Kai governor, there was a large earthquake as the lava reached the lakes. The lava spilt into Lake Motosu and Senoumi, boiling the water and killing all the marine life inside. The villagers who lived in the area were buried by the lava as it stormed down the mountain; more people than they could count. It was a disaster unlike any they had ever seen, and countless lives perished.

As the lava rolled down the mountain, it consumed everything in its way. Thousands of trees were buried, burning in the hot lava. Many of these trees created what is known as tree moulds; as the lava hardened, it did so in the shape of the tree that was burning inside it. Modern day researchers have used these tree moulds to uncover what type of trees formerly grew in the area, extracting pieces of bark that survived in the hardened lava. The forest that used to exist where present-day Aokigahara grows was full of Japanese firs and other needle-leaved trees. It's thought this former forest was subarctic, and these firs now only grow close to Mount Fuji's summit, which is snow-capped for close to half the year.

The continual eruptions sent more and more lava down the mountain, which then hardened on top of the existing lava. This, along with the tree moulds, is what created the numerous tunnels and caves found in Aokigahara today. This includes some of Aokigahara's most popular tourist attractions, such as the Fugaku Wind Cave and Narusawa Ice Cave. You can also find an area close to the outskirts of Aokigahara called the Koori Ana Crater Line. *Koori Ana* roughly translates to "ice holes." This crater line was formed during the Jougan eruptions, one of the many sites that split and sent curtains of fire into the air. Craters and holes like this can be found all over Aokigahara, making it extremely treacherous to navigate.

And what of Senoumi? After all, no such lake exists anymore. Did the lava entirely fill it in? Not really. As the Kai governor stated in his report to the Royal Court, Senoumi was filled with lava and split in two. The lakes we now know as Shoji and Saiko, two of the Fuji Five Lakes, are all that's left of that former body of water. They were once joined, and much larger in size, but there was so much lava that it filled most of the lake in, leaving two much smaller bodies of water in its wake. Radiocarbon dating has confirmed that Shoji and Saiko were indeed once Senoumi, split by the Jougan eruption. However, they might not be as separate as they seem. Although separated by a distance of several kilometres, it's thought that somewhere underneath all that hardened lava there is a tunnel. The water levels of both lakes always remain the same, suggesting they are still linked deep below the surface.

There is an area just outside of Aokigahara Forest called Oshino Hakkai. It consists of eight beautiful ponds that attract many tourists who wish to see their beauty year in, year out. Some years back, two divers went into one of the ponds to investigate the tunnels within their walls. These ponds were formed in another eruption that took place roughly 60 years before the Jougan eruption. After entering, the divers never returned. A robot was sent in the next day to retrieve their dead bodies. It was assumed they got lost in the tunnels and were unable to find their way out. They drowned, despite the fact the pond was only five metres wide and five metres deep. The extent of the tunnel network created by the eruptions is still unknown, and can prove deadly even for trained professionals.

The Jougan eruption took place nearly 1,200 years ago. After the mountain stopped spewing fire, it left nothing but desolation behind. From Mount Nagao on Fuji's side, all the way down to the remains of Senoumi, everything was covered in hardened lava. This lava cannot hold water, but something else can: moss.

Mount Fuji ceased erupting, and life slowly returned to the area. Marine life returned to the lakes, and people set about resettling the surrounding areas. Roughly 400 years after the

Jougan eruption, moss started growing over the hardened lava remains. Moss can hold water, and where there's a will, there's a way. Seeds found their way into the moss, most likely thanks to passing birds, and, roughly 900 years after the Jougan eruption, the first trees began to grow. Around this same time, Mount Fuji erupted again, this time in what is known as the Hoei eruption. This eruption was only half the size of the Jougan one and took place on the opposite side of the mountain, on the southeast side. It only released ash, as opposed to lava, and this ash release flew east of Mount Fuji, away from the burgeoning forest and towards Tokyo. The trees were safe.

The oldest known tree in Aokigahara has been dated to 300 years ago. This particular tree is located on the outskirts of the forest, which has led researchers to believe that this was one of the first areas to grow. The trees then spread further inside, eventually encompassing an area of up to 40 square kilometres that is now called Aokigahara. Even in this most desolate of regions, an area where seemingly nothing would ever grow again, nature found a way.

2. WHAT'S IN A NAME?

DIRECTLY TRANSLATED, AOKIGAHARA means "field of green trees." It's said it got its name because looking down upon Aokigahara from up high was like looking upon a vast sea of green trees. *Ao* meaning blue or green, *ki* meaning trees, and *hara* meaning field, or when used in the word *unabara*, an ocean. It is also from this that we get its popular nickname *jukai*, which literally means "a sea of trees." While Aokigahara Jukai is not the forest's official name, you can still find it written on maps and many people refer to it as such. Many simply call the area "Jukai," and there's no confusion as to where that's referring to. A great deal of media produced about the forest uses the term "Jukai" because it's shorter, more concise, and packs more punch. A sea of trees sounds dark and foreboding. A field a green trees, not so much.

Within Aokigahara you'll find so many trees packed densely together that even during midday it's dim, dark, and full of shadows. Sunlight has trouble penetrating the vast ocean of branches above, and the little that gets through casts an eerie glow over the area. Thanks to the hardened lava that the forest has grown over, the ground is extremely uneven and treacherous. Moss grows over everything, and the forest floor is riddled with unseen holes, cave openings, and tunnels. Many of these are hidden beneath rotten branches and dead trees; even if one attempts to traverse the forest with the utmost caution, danger lurks with each step.

The trees that grow in the forest now are

predominantly pines and broad-leaved trees. Winter reaches below freezing in Aokigahara thanks to its elevation on Mount Fuji, but in summer it's humid. Extremely humid. This causes the trees to rot and fall apart like sand. Their base is very shallow, consisting only of a thin covering of moss and whatever trees have died before them. This makes it difficult for trees to grow old, because the older they get, the larger they get. The larger they get, the more they weigh, and in the sticky humidity of summer many are unable to hold on. Their tangled roots which snake across the ground aren't enough to hold them up any longer and they fall, rotting on the ground and joining the circle of life as the next seeds sprout in their remains.

When you think of Aokigahara, two different images might come to mind. One of those may be the view of Aokigahara from above, the eponymous Sea of Trees that seems to spread out forever in all directions. The other, and perhaps stronger image, is of the twisted tree roots that snake their way across the ground.

The moss and dirt that cover the hardened lava is only about two centimetres high. Think about that for a moment. If you plant a seed in two centimetres of dirt, keep it in the shade and ensure the only water it has access to is from the surrounding moss, you're probably not going to end up with the healthiest, strongest plant. Now imagine 40 square kilometres of forest growing in those same conditions. The roots have nowhere to go, and so they snake outward, over the moss and through each other, making the already dangerous terrain even more so. This is one of Aokigahara's most iconic features, something that makes it instantly distinguishable in photos. The moss then spreads over the roots and up the base of the trees, painting not just the roof of the forest green, but the floor as well.

3. LOCATING THE FOREST

AOKIGAHARA'S OFFICIAL ADDRESS is Narusawa, Fujikawaguchiko, Minamitsuru District, Yamanashi Prefecture, 401-0300, Japan. Perhaps owing to its popularity as a suicide spot, people may have the image that the forest is difficult to reach, which couldn't be further from the truth. The fact is, Aokigahara is a massive forest on Mount Fuji, the largest mountain in Japan, and one of the most popular tourist destinations for both locals and foreigners alike.

There are numerous tourist spots in and around the area, so access via public transport is the easiest and most common method. If you're going by train, the closest station is Kawaguchiko Station. From there, you can take the Saiko Round Trip bus (green line) for 30 minutes, which will drop you off at Saiko Koumori Ana Mae, one of the more popular drop-off points for the forest. There are also numerous highway buses that stop at Kawaguchiko Station, where you can again change to the Saiko Round Trip bus.

If you're going by car, National Highway 139 will get you there, and if you want to go even further in, Prefectural Highway 71 cuts right through the middle of the forest. Yes, despite being a virgin forest, Aokigahara is far from untouched, and not only does a rather large highway cut the forest in half, but you can find numerous roads and settlements around the outskirts. It's not just a tourist spot; people live there.

It might seem strange if you've never been there,

and even more so if your image of Aokigahara is simply "the suicide forest," but a short distance away you can find a giant amusement park called Fuji-Q Highland. It's famous for its many roller coasters, and people come from all over the country to visit it. A few kilometres to the southwest you can find Fuji Subaruland, a theme park for the whole family to enjoy that just recently celebrated its 50th anniversary. The lakes surrounding Aokigahara are famous for fishing and camping, and see a high volume of both tourists and locals during the warmer months. There are also numerous lodgings around the lakes for tourists who aren't after the authentic camping experience, but would rather relax in full modern comfort instead.

Perhaps the most popular "final destination" before entering Aokigahara is the Fugaku Wind Cave parking lot. From here, both Fugaku Wind Cave and Narusawa Ice Cave, arguably the two most popular tourist destinations within Aokigahara, can be reached. There is another smaller parking lot closer to Narusawa Ice Cave, but the Fugaku Wind Cave parking lot is much larger and houses a small shop wherein you can grab food, drinks, and souvenirs before heading in. Their corn flavoured ice cream is especially popular. During holidays and weekends this area can become particularly crowded, and it's not uncommon to see large groups of tourists and school groups nearby. You might even hear those kids talking about rumours of dead bodies hanging from trees inside the forest, and disbelief from their more suspicious friends...

For many, the last convenience store on the way to Aokigahara is the 7-Eleven on National Highway 139. This means that it's also the last convenience store for the many visitors to Aokigahara who plan to never leave again. Plastic bags bearing the 7-Eleven logo are often found close to bodies discovered in the forest. Unlike the usual bright 7-Eleven colours you may be used to, this particular store sports a black logo. When you realise that many people buy their final meal from here, the darkness of the logo becomes even more sombre. And what do people tend to buy from 7-Eleven as their final meal before entering Aokigahara? Bags discovered near bodies have revealed stamina drinks, cigarettes, fried chicken, and full bento meals... often uneaten and still in their wrapping.

WHY DO PEOPLE GO THERE TO DIE?

AT 11:15 P.M. ON MARCH 13, 2004, a family of three pulled into an empty lot near Saiko Lake. The father, a 56-year-old unemployed man, drove, while the daughter, a 30-year-old unemployed woman, sat in the passenger's seat. The mother, a 54-year-old woman who was also unemployed, sat in the rear behind her. They were about to take part in what is referred to as a forced double suicide. The parents strangled their daughter with a strap from a shoulder bag, and then the father entered the forest and hung himself. The mother attempted to hang herself as well, but when that didn't work, she returned to the car and attempted to fill it with gas. When this also didn't work, she gave in and called the police. When the police arrived, she revealed the family was drowning in debt, and so the parents decided that suicide was the only option, and they would take their daughter with them. The father was found shortly thereafter and confirmed dead. Only the mother survived. The family were from Kansai.

At 7:50 a.m. on November 16, the same year, a 40-year-old government worker was discovered in his car roughly 500 metres from Owada Incineration Plant in Aokigahara. His three-year-old daughter was discovered in the car with him, indicating yet another forced double suicide. The man was from Gunma.

Statistics from 2008 suggested that close to 8,000 people a year committed suicide because of financial reasons, and many of them went to Aokigahara to do so. This became such a common problem that a billboard was erected within the forest stating "We can help you settle your debts!" Many of the people who committed suicide were saddled with debt from loan sharks and other illegal gangs and saw suicide as the only way out.

Within a year of being erected, 29 people had called the phone number listed on the sign to get help. One woman from Tokyo called the line and was reported as saying, "I'm thinking of committing suicide. I've hung a rope around the tree and I'm about to hang myself." The woman had borrowed more than 2,500,000 yen from five different loan shark companies and had been struggling to pay them back for over 10 years. The person on the other end informed her, "You've overpaid what you owe, you don't have to pay anything else now. We can get that extra money back, but you mustn't die." The woman was saved, but not all are so lucky.

People come to visit Aokigahara from all over looking to end their pain. Not all are suffering from debt, and not all decide to make that last call for help. But how did Aokigahara, a beautiful virgin forest with long spiritual ties, become a beacon for those hoping to end their lives? What drove more and more people to end their suffering in this one particular spot? There are forests all over Japan, many of them dark and dangerous and located in far less busy locations than Aokigahara. Mount Fuji is one of the most popular tourist spots in all of Japan, and the caves within Aokigahara see thousands upon thousands of tourists each year. It's a busy area all year round, so what draws people to it?

4. NOVEL BEGINNINGS

FROM MAY 29, 1959, to June 15, 1960, popular magazine *Josei Jishin* published a serial by author Matsumoto Seichou called *Nami no Tou*. This story was collected and published as a novel in the same year and was so popular that it also became a television drama. The novel tells the story of Yoriko, a housewife who falls in love with a young public prosecutor. Their love is not to be, however. The young prosecutor promises to give up his career and run away with Yoriko, and they agree to meet at Tokyo Station. But, thinking of the young man's future, Yoriko instead goes to Shinjuku, getting on the train and heading towards Aokigahara. She stops at a youth hostel near the forest for one final coffee, and then exits, heading down a lone path into the forest. An old couple working in a field nearby end the novel with a brief yet chilling conversation.

"If you go down that path, you'll never return again."

"Oh my, that woman, she just ran down the road."

"Lies. You're just seeing things. I told her that same thing just now, there's no way she'd go down there."

The heartbreaking fate of these star-crossed lovers touched the hearts of readers all around the country. Yoriko and her lover may have been fiction, but Aokigahara was real. The youth hostel

Yoriko visited at the end of the book was real. The path she walked down as she entered the forest to end her own life was real. Matsumoto himself visited the youth hostel while researching for his book, and he walked down that lone, dark path into the forest, long boots on and a rope tied around his waist. This rope connected him to some watchful locals who made sure he didn't get lost on the way. The taxi driver who drove Matsumoto there still remembers him to this day. After the book came out, people began to refer to that path as "the one Yoriko took to enter the forest."

In 1974, the skeleton of a woman was discovered inside Aokigahara. Beside her they found the book *Nami no Tou*. This woman is considered by many to be the first person in modern times to take their life in what would become known as the Suicide Forest. After the cultural impact of *Nami no Tou*, it was as if this woman's death opened the flood gates, so to speak, and more and more people began to seek the forest out to end their lives as well. *Nami no Tou* was discovered by yet another body in 1985. But can one single book truly be to blame? Could one fictional novel have resulted in thousands of people travelling from all over the country to end their lives in one particular forest?

Statistically, it's near impossible that this woman was the first person to ever take her own life inside Aokigahara. She may have been the first publicised in the media, and the discovery of *Nami no Tou* by her side can only be seen as part of her decision to go to this exact forest, but she was not the first person in history, nor even modern history, to choose Aokigahara to end her life. The problem with providing hard proof, however, lies in the fact that death records from the area don't ever specify Aokigahara as the place of death. Instead, they record the village names within Aokigahara. Even if a body was found inside the forest itself, it is attributed to the nearby village instead.

Locals have long viewed the forest as a dangerous and terrifying place. One woman in her 80s was quoted as saying that when she was a child, she was warned that if she ever entered the forest, she would never come back. Children were taught early to fear it, perhaps because of how naturally dangerous it was. The uneven ground, slippery moss, and tangled roots mean that you can feel like you've walked several hundred metres, when in reality you've only walked 10 or 20. Everything looks the same, and walking a mere 10 metres off track can see you lost and unable to find your way out again. Combined with the numerous caves, tunnels, and other pitfalls built into the hardened lava, it's not really a place for adults to be wandering around in blindly, let alone children. It does, however, make the forest the perfect place to disappear, if that is your desire. Yet another good reason to keep children out. This particular woman would have been a child around the 1920s and 30s, long before *Nami no Tou* came out.

In the early 2000s, Hayano Azusa, a geologist who has been studying Aokigahara for several decades now, visited the forest with a photographer friend who was hoping to capture some animals within it. Before long they happened upon an old, white skull. It was small, perhaps that of a woman or child, and the first Hayano had ever seen with moss growing on it. Hayano has worked in Aokigahara for a long time, and discovered numerous bodies in varying states of decay during that time. Even though it was only a skull, the pair still called the police. The police wrapped matters up quickly and attempted to leave, but something about the situation bothered him. Where was the rest of the body? The position of the skull signified that the person had died on that very spot, but the body was nowhere to be seen.

The officers returned and, at Hayano's urging, dug around the tree. They found nothing but tree roots. Still not satisfied, Hayano asked them to dig *under* the tree. They found the rest of the skeleton, the tree growing up over it. When the person died, they had died on a slope. Dirt and old leaves eventually piled over the body as it decayed and then a seed took root. The tree grew up over the corpse. It was fully grown by the time Hayano and his friend found it, and the skull covered in moss. That body had been there for a long time. Well before *Nami no Tou*'s influence.

They say that the topography within Aokigahara changes approximately every 50 years. The reason for this is that the trees grow, become large and unable to support their own weight, then fall down and cover the ground, rotting until new life forms on top of that. Unless you know exactly what you're looking for, or as in Hayano's case, you happen to get lucky, things can remain buried beneath the constantly changing landscape for eternity…

There are old paths within Aokigahara left by those who once tried to reclaim the land. In the 1950s and 60s, logging companies moved in to transport timber from the forest, but the difficult conditions soon put an end to that. They were hardly the first, however, and for as long as the forest has been there, people have been trying to tame it. People have discovered old cooking stoves, stone walls, and even monuments from people who in times past tried to make a living there. Elderly locals speak of families who tried to reclaim the land back when they were small children. Despite their best efforts, the forest is a harsh mistress and unsuitable for farming, raising animals, or anything else necessary to sustain life. One elderly man spoke of how an entire family once disappeared into the forest after their failed efforts and were never seen again, much like the forced family suicides mentioned at the beginning of this chapter.

Times were particularly hard after Japan's loss at the end of World War II. When the soldiers returned home, they faced constant gossip and people talking behind their backs wherever they went. Many had nowhere to go, and so they withdrew from society. Many more contemplated suicide.

When you think of the beauty of nature in Japan, what comes to mind? Chances are good that Mount Fuji is at least one of those places, and for a person looking to disappear from society, or end their life surrounded by the beauty they fought so hard for, that giant sea of trees sitting on its side no doubt sounds like a great place to start.

Elderly locals who still live in the area reported

that many soldiers disappeared into the forest after the war and never came back out again. Perhaps this too is why children were warned never to go in there. Why they were warned the forest was "scary." Why they were warned that if you went in, you would never come back out. Aokigahara has long been known as a place you don't want to enter if you ever have plans of coming out again. This history goes way, way back. Much longer than *Nami no Tou*.

5. THE PRACTICE OF UBASUTE

THERE HAVE LONG been rumours that Aokigahara was used for the practice of *ubasute*. Ubasute literally means "throwing away the elderly." It's an old custom of abandoning the elderly to die in the mountains, usually because times are tough and the family can no longer support them. There are no official records of ubasute ever having taken place, but tales of it have been passed down through the ages as folklore. Some have suggested that it was just an idea, a story, an old urban legend, if you will. Others, however, believe that it did take place, but in very small numbers. It was not a widespread practice, but something that was only done in desperate times of need. Some have argued that Aokigahara was actually the birthplace of the practice, although not all agree.

In the 2016 movie *The Forest* (released in Japan as *Jukai*), Mount Fuji is treated as an *ubasute yama*, a mountain where people abandon the elderly to die. One of the ghosts within Aokigahara is an elderly woman who was one such victim of the practice, and as you can probably imagine, she isn't happy about it. The quality of the movie aside, it is true—according to the legends, of course—that the practice of ubasute did once take place on Mount Fuji.

There is a cave referred to as the "ubasute cave" that was formed when Mount Fuji erupted long ago. Most call it *banba ana*, or "the old lady hole" in English. This hole is not actually located within Aokigahara, but to the southwest of Mount Fuji;

meaning it was created in a different eruption to the one that created Aokigahara. It's roughly one metre wide and 10 metres deep (although the depth can vary depending on who you talk to). These days it's covered in barbed wire to keep people from falling in, but legend has it that the hole was used to dispose of the elderly during particularly tough times in the Edo Period. And, if you believe ghost hunters, the spirit of an old lady often appears near the hole. Ghostly hands are said to reach out and grab passersby, pulling them into its dark depths. Numerous stories litter the internet of people's encounters with the supernatural at banba ana; all anonymous or heard from friends of a friend, of course.

An investigation of the cave discovered there *were* bones inside; chicken bones, in addition to human. The bones were thought to belong to a person from the Edo period. It's important to remember that the cave is a giant hole in the ground, and these were the only bones discovered. If the cave really was used to dispose of the elderly, one might imagine there would be more bones in it. But, it is a giant hole in the ground. It's not hard to imagine someone stumbling over the hole during the course of its history and falling inside, unable to get back out again. Was the so-called ubasute cave actually used to get rid of the elderly? It's unlikely, but the story is a popular one.

There's another cave to the north that also goes by the same name (differentiated by using different kanji). This one is also accompanied by a sad tale of elderly abandonment, but tales of the two "banba anas" often get mixed up because they share the same name and general location. And yes, according to the rumours, this one is haunted as well.

Neither of these caves are in Aokigahara, but they are close. This, combined with stories of how Mount Fuji may have been used to abandon the elderly in the past, make Aokigahara the perfect ubasute setting. After all, you just have to travel perhaps 20 or 30 metres in, leave the elderly person there, and then find your way back out (if you can…). Aokigahara is difficult to traverse even if you are young, healthy, and outfitted with the best modern technology to guide your way. For a weak, starved, elderly person during the Edo period? Near impossible.

However, we cannot state with any certainty that the practice of ubasute ever took place at Aokigahara. The practice itself has only been passed down to us through folklore, and there is no hard evidence that it was ever a real thing. Is it possible that families abandoned the elderly (with or without their consent) in the forest when times were tough? Of course. Is there any evidence that it actually took place? There isn't. All we have are stories and folklore, and neither of these are proof. They do add to the forest's never-ending mystique, though. The mystique that may have helped *Nami no Tou* come about.

6. TEMPTATION OF THE FOREST

BEFORE THE 1960S, Aokigahara wasn't known as the Suicide Forest. It was scary, yes, and it was difficult to traverse, but when people heard the word "Aokigahara" they didn't immediately associate it with "Suicide Forest." That changed with *Nami no Tou*, and as later movies and TV dramas were created, it became even more popular. After that first woman's body was discovered with *Nami no Tou* by her side, others quickly followed suit. The mass media picked up on it and began reporting Aokigahara as a "suicide spot," which then became a self-fulfilling prophecy. It was known as a suicide spot, so people travelled there to die. The more people who died there, the more its fame spread. It was always seen as a scary place, but now, people were heading there in droves to kill themselves. It was a vicious circle.

For those who make it their job (or hobby) to study Aokigahara, one of the first questions they are often asked is "Why?" Why are people drawn to Aokigahara when looking to end their pain? Many answer "*Nami no Tou*." The NHK drama in 1973 was especially popular, and most suicides in the forest started after it aired. But there are those who claim Aokigahara was famous as a suicide spot even before that, and it was for that reason that Matsumoto, the author, chose Aokigahara as the location of the book's dramatic final act.

Let's take a look at the facts. Aokigahara is quite a large distance from many of Japan's biggest cities. It's roughly 120 km from Tokyo, nearly 400 km from Osaka, and about 250 km from Nagoya. That's in a straight line using modern highways. Even if we remove cars from the equation and assume the same direct route, it would take several days—at least—to walk from one of the major cities to Aokigahara. That's assuming good weather and no obstacles or detours on the way.

What about trains, you say? Kawaguchiko, the closest station to Aokigahara, didn't open until 1950, and even so, it's still a further 30 minute bus ride from there to the forest. If we assume that it was a famous suicide spot before *Nami no Tou*, it was still a difficult one to reach. That's not to say it may not have had that reputation with the locals, but in terms of Aokigahara's now worldwide fame as a suicide forest, it's a difficult hypothesis to swallow. If someone was healthy enough to make the trip all the way from Tokyo (the closest of the big cities) to Aokigahara because of its infamy, they probably wouldn't be travelling there to kill themselves in the first place. Suicide spots exist all over Japan; it's much easier to go to a closer one instead.

After household cars became more common, public transport improved, and Mount Fuji boomed as a tourist location, it became much easier to access Aokigahara. Perhaps coincidentally, this all happened around the same time as the *Nami no Tou* boom. So why were people drawn there? Japan is full of suicide spots. Places like the Chuo Line in Tokyo, the Bay Bridge in Yokohama, the Tojinbo cliffs in Fukui, and Kegon Falls in Tochigi; each prefecture has its own famous "suicide spot" that people can reach more easily than Aokigahara, and yet, people still travel all that way. Why?

Aokigahara is not an easy or painless place to die in. "But you just spent all this time talking about how treacherous and dangerous the forest is!" Yes, and somewhat ironically, if you are looking to commit suicide, Aokigahara is *not* the easiest place for it. The ground is uneven and covered in moss, making it difficult to enter. It's full of tourists and there are many walking paths and picnic areas for the numerous people that pass through it day in, day out. The trees are literally clinging on for dear life, meaning that a great deal of them will fall over if you try to hang a rope around them, or the branch will snap straight off. Chances are good that you'll injure yourself before you're able to go through with the act, leaving you to die slowly of injury, weakness, or starvation instead. People are also well aware of Aokigahara's reputation nowadays, and many are on the lookout for those who may be intending to take their own life. Others search the forest rigorously for the same reason, or simply because they enjoy it. So again, you might ask, "Why?"

Because everybody else does.

This is something that all major suicide spots around the world have in common. It's that vicious circle we spoke of earlier. People commit suicide there, so it makes the news. More people hear of it and decide to go there for the same reason. The circle continues. The Mapo Bridge in Seoul, South Korea, is one such location. A campaign began in 2012 to reduce the number of people who killed themselves by jumping from the bridge. It had the opposite effect, however, and the attention it drew to the bridge saw a sixfold increase in jumpers. Why did they do it? Because thanks to the campaign, people's associations of the bridge as a suicide spot were solidified. More people heard about it, perhaps for the first time, and when contemplating suicide, Mapo Bridge was the first place that came to mind. Aokigahara is no different.

There's one more factor to consider when it comes to Aokigahara's fame as a suicide spot; its inclusion in the 1993 publication *The Complete Manual of Suicide*. We can't lay all the blame on *Nami no Tou*. *The Complete Manual of Suicide* caused quite a stir when it was released. As you might expect from the title, the book details different methods of suicide, how best to go about them, and includes information like how painful a particular method may be. Several prefectures restricted sale of the book to under 18s, and many argued that the book itself was contributing to Japan's high suicide rates. One section of the book includes suicide spots from around the country, in which Aokigahara is listed. *Nami no Tou* wasn't the only book discovered next to dead bodies inside the forest; many more were found with *The Complete Manual of Suicide*, or at the very least, the torn out pages featuring Aokigahara.

The book details Aokigahara as "a place in which you will never be found." Of course, just like Mapo Bridge in Seoul, this had the opposite effect. Even more people went to Aokigahara, thinking it a good spot to end their lives. This made it even more popular than before. Popularity brings people; both those looking to kill themselves, and those trying to stop them. After the book was released, people reported finding up to four bodies a day when searching the forest. In recent years, the book's influence has begun to die down, but it played a huge part in the "Aokigahara boom" of the 90s and 2000s.

7. SEARCH PARTIES

1978: 42	1985: 37	1992: 21	1999: 68
1979: 48	1986: 40	1993: 39	2000: 59
1980: 26	1987: 28	1994: 57	2001: 59
1981: 25	1988: 21	1995: 53	2002: 78
1982: 31	1989: 53	1996: 44	2003: 105
1983: 38	1990: 31	1997: 55	2004: 108
1984: 25	1991: 21	1998: 73	

Bodies discovered in Aokigahara

IN 1959, MATSUMOTO Seichou published *Nami no Tou*. After this, the number of suicides within Aokigahara began to rise. There's no official data from this time, but in 1971, the local Fujiyoshida police department organised the first of what would become annual search parties. 390 police officers, fire fighters, and other volunteers set out at 8 in the morning. By the time they returned at 11 a.m., they had discovered four bodies.

The purpose of these search parties was twofold. First, with the increasing number of suicides taking place in the forest, these mass searches hoped to find those who had taken their own lives and, hopefully, return their bodies to their families to be laid to rest. Second, it was an attempt at suicide prevention. You might be wondering how a search party would prevent someone from taking their life inside the forest, but it's important to think of the reasons *why* people go there to do it.

As *The Complete Manual of Suicide* states, you can disappear in Aokigahara and never be found again. The reason many Japanese people choose

Aokigahara is because of the shame their death would bring upon their family. Many simply wish to disappear entirely. They don't want people finding and viewing their corpse after death. It is a private moment, their last with nature and themselves, and they do not want to be found. With these searches the police were, in essence, broadcasting their intent to uncover those bodies and return them to civilisation. Their bodies *would* be found. People *would* see their corpses and what they went through in their final moments. Their bodies would be removed from what they hoped would be their final resting place, hidden away from the world they no longer wished to live in, and returned to their families. It was a message. If you don't want your final moments uncovered, if you don't want us involving your family after your death, then don't come here. You can no longer freely disappear from the world. We will find you, and we will keep looking until we do.

Taking place in October of each year, right as the weather starts to cool, these search parties tended to uncover close to seven or eight bodies each time. The search parties occasionally came into contact with those looking to end their lives as well. These people were taken into their care and removed from the forest. However, despite their best efforts, these search parties did little to end the rising number of suicides within Aokigahara. In fact, so many bodies were uncovered over the years that the Fujiyoshida Police Station had to construct a separate building to house them all.

For those who wished to remain unknown after

death, they were careful to enter the forest without anything identifiable on them. This meant leaving all ID and personal items behind. Particularly in the summer months, the rapid speed of decay meant that within a few short weeks it would be near impossible to identify a body. While investigating the deceased—which must be done with each and every person discovered, no matter how recent or old the corpse is—they are kept on-site at Fujiyoshida Police Station. If the remains are identified, they are quickly returned to family who must then foot the burial expenses. If the remains are unidentifiable, however, they remain at Fujiyoshida until cremation can be arranged, and the bill is then footed by the local government. Yet another reason many did not wish to be found; if they were, and their body identified, their family would be forced to cover all the costs of their death, which could reach up to 100,000 yen, or roughly US$1,000.

Yet, in 2001, it was announced that these search parties would be ending, exactly 30 years after they began. The official reason was that they were drawing too much attention to Aokigahara. Each year the search parties uncovered numerous bodies, and this was reported in the news. Once more, people nationwide were reminded that Aokigahara was a massive suicide spot and people were still going there to do it. The searches were having the opposite effect; as stated earlier, the more people became aware of Aokigahara as a suicide spot, the more they were drawn to it. Numbers continued to rise over the years, rarely dropping below 50. It was hoped that by ending the official search parties, less attention would be drawn to Aokigahara and people would stop associating it with suicide. But, as you can see from the numbers above, the plan didn't work.

The Japanese economic bubble crashed in the early 90s, and economic stagnation set in. Although officials tried to stop drawing attention to Aokigahara, the recession took hold and people continued to the forest in droves to end their lives, unable to see a way out of the crisis. The number of bodies discovered each year after the cancellation of the search parties rose so dramatically that in 2005, Yamanashi Prefecture stopped announcing them entirely. By that point, the number had reached over 100 for several years in a row, nearly twice that of previous decades. The vicious circle seemed unending. Yamanashi Prefecture then decided to change tracks.

In June 2008, the local government and police department formed the Sustaining Life Aokigahara Network Council. The family of a man who had committed suicide in the forest donated 5 million yen the previous year to fund the placement of security cameras in nearby parking lots and stores. It was hoped that this would help prevent people from entering the forest, knowing that they would be caught on camera beforehand.

In November 2008, the council then proposed hiring volunteers to patrol Aokigahara and call out to those who they suspected weren't regular tourists. These people ranged from taxi and bus drivers, to shop workers and concerned locals. Over

100 people agreed to participate. Unlike the search parties, which took place once a year, these volunteers would constantly be on the lookout and hoping to catch people before they disappeared, not after. These volunteers still patrol the area to this day, but with official numbers no longer being released, it's difficult to judge how successful they've been at preventing suicides.

8. THE SUICIDE ZONE

AOKIGAHARA IS A big place. People often say that once you go in, you'll never come back out again. If you're looking to end your life somewhere where your body will never be found, Aokigahara is a good bet. Taking the largest general estimate of the forest, that's a good 40 square kilometres to work with. Bodies like the one geologist Hayano Azusa discovered could be lying in the forest for decades before anyone finds them. And yet, despite this mass of untamed forest, the great majority of suicides take place within the same tiny area. An area that Aokigahara aficionados have dubbed the *danchi*, or the suicide zone.

The word *danchi* literally means a housing complex or apartment building. So many people take their lives in this one area that it's basically a housing complex for the dead. It's morbid, yes, but for the people who make it their hobby to uncover dead bodies within the forest, it fits with their black humour.

The *danchi* is an area located between Narusawa Ice Cave and Fugaku Wind Cave. There is a path within the forest that takes about 20 minutes on foot from one cave to the other. Here you can take a leisurely stroll, sit on a bench to enjoy the scenery, and listen to the cars as they drive past on the nearby Highway 139. However, despite its idyllic beauty, just past the trees lie the remains of many who took their own lives. About halfway between Narusawa Ice Cave and Fugaku Wind Cave, there is a path that branches off to the south. Access is now blocked to the public with a "forbidden entry" sign, but either side of this particular path is one of the most common areas to find bodies.

The area otherwise known as the *danchi* is well-trafficked. Tourists stroll along the path day in, day out, enjoying the forest while a busy national highway is only a few hundred metres away. Why, of all places, do people choose this particular spot to take their lives?

Geologist Hayano Azusa noted that he took a scientist who specialised in studies of the human brain into the forest. After walking around for a while, the scientist told Hayano that he wanted to see the area where most people commit suicide. Hayano took him to the *danchi*, and the scientist nodded his head in agreement. "I see, you can still hear the sounds of civilisation here," he remarked. "Even in the end, people are still driven by their three base desires."

These three base desires are the desire for food, sex, and community. He theorised that people were unconsciously drawn to the area because, even in the end, they still wanted to be close to civilisation. To community. Aokigahara is a big, scary place. It doesn't take long to wander off the path and get lost in its dark confines. Yet, the simple act of hearing cars in the distance can be a relief. In one's final moments, they are not truly alone. There are others nearby, even if they don't know they are there. That, the scientist suggested, could be a comfort to many.

Furthermore, most people looking to commit suicide in the forest don't travel there by car or bike. Once abandoned, these vehicles quickly become suspicious to locals, and a simple registration check will show who it belongs to. The great majority of people travelling this far to end their lives don't want people to know they are there. They want to disappear. An abandoned car or motorcycle will immediately tip off police that the owner is likely somewhere inside, and lead to a search for them. As such, most people enter the forest via public transport, and if you're coming by public transport, two of the easiest places to get off are at Narusawa Ice Cave and Fugaku Wind Cave. Everybody gets off there. You can blend in, and you don't leave a suspicious vehicle behind that can give away your identity.

Without that private transport, you're limited to public. Most of Aokigahara is quite difficult to enter from the outside, so people who are new to the forest aren't likely to get far, leaving them a little too close to the community for comfort. It's no coincidence that most people end up in the same area. It just makes sense. The majority of bodies are discovered only 100 metres from the path in the danchi (and about 300~500 metres from the highway). It's a struggle to go much further, and even for a pro, traversing 100 metres of Aokigahara terrain is no easy feat. Thus, many are found only 50~75 metres from the path. Reaching this distance can take a lot of energy, and you might feel like you've been walking for hours, even though you haven't actually covered much distance.

Scholars have also proposed one more theory about why the danchi, or suicide zone, is so popular.

If all the above weren't enough, there is one other factor that plays an important part in someone's decision for where to spend their final moments in life: tranquillity. The trees open up towards the sky, allowing more sunlight in and casting a peaceful, warm glow over the area. The ground becomes somewhat flatter, and many of the trees are large, thick, and sturdy compared to those closer to the path. This is also important for another reason... Many ropes are found hanging from these trees, as they are some of the few strong enough to hold a human body without snapping.

If you want to get deeper into the forest without anyone knowing you're there, then taking public transport, following the existing path in, and then heading off the beaten track is the easiest way to do it. The area is peaceful, the trees are strong, and the sounds of civilisation can be heard not too far away. And, similar to Aokigahara the popular suicide spot becoming a self-fulfilling prophecy, the more people who hear about the *danchi*, the more people that head there themselves.

9. UNCOVERING THE BODIES

YOU'RE WALKING THROUGH Aokigahara when it finally happens. You've heard about it happening to other people, but never once expected that it would happen to you. You've stumbled across a body. Now what do you do?

Despite what you may have been led to believe, it's not all that common to just happen upon a body inside Aokigahara. There are groups of Aokigahara aficionados—sometimes referred to in Japanese as having "Aokigahara mania"—who dedicate their free time to combing the forest to find these bodies. Their reasons are their own, and they're often not pretty. One especially infamous aficionado, usually referred to as "K-san" in media related to the forest, has been exploring Aokigahara for decades now. This all stemmed from an incident several decades ago where he took part in a search party and stumbled across a decaying body. Rather than disgusting him, he found himself intrigued by it, and has ever since spent his time trying to find more. Murata Ramu—a writer with decades of Aokigahara experience himself—has described him as "the scariest man in Aokigahara."

Yet even for K-san, and his fellow Aokigahara maniacs, stumbling across a body isn't as easy as it seems. Many searches turn up nothing at all. Groups of people can search the forest all day and find nothing. It is a big place, difficult to traverse, and more efforts than ever have been put into stopping suicidal people before they enter. But just because it's uncommon, it doesn't mean that it never happens. So, what happens when somebody discovers a dead body inside Aokigahara?

The first point of call is, of course, the police. This isn't always as easy as it sounds. Much of the forest is out of range for cell phones, meaning you'll have to travel to one of the few areas where you can get reception. Not only will this take time, but you'll need to leave the body where it is, meaning you could potentially lose its location. It's recommended that people carry *suzuran* tape when travelling off the tourist paths. This is a type of coloured plastic that's cut thin like tape. You can tie one end to a tree and more safely navigate your way through the forest, then follow the tape back when you're done.

Aokigahara is full of suzuran tape, so much so that locals have complained of it destroying the beauty of the forest. People tie it to trees and then leave it there when they're done. This piles up over time, leaving the forest covered in colourful tape that adventurers don't think to take home, destroying the natural beauty of the place. Think of a yard covered in streamers from a long, boisterous party. Popular areas of Aokigahara can look just like that if not regularly cleaned up by volunteers.

Regardless, if you are travelling off the designated paths, it's a good idea to carry suzuran tape with you. You can't always rely on someone else leaving theirs behind, especially with all the efforts to keep Aokigahara clean these days. Tying this to a tree and finding your way back to an area with reception is your first port of call. Once you find reception, it might be tempting to immediately call the police, but stop and think. Can you describe to the police where you are? How are they supposed to find you? "I'm near Fugaku Wind Cave" covers a massive area, and everything looks the same. Experts recommend finding something that stands out and then giving as detailed instructions as you can. "I'm roughly this many kilometres from Fugaku Wind Cave on the way to Narusawa Ice Cave. I'm standing by three wooden benches and wearing a yellow coat," for example.

Calling 110, Japan's emergency number, will put you through to the Yamanashi police. From there, they will take your number and forward it to the local station—Fujiyoshida—who will then call you back to get the details. This can take some time, so don't panic if they don't call back immediately. They will ask the condition of the body, whether there are any personal effects, and other questions of this nature. This information is used so the police know how many and which personnel to bring. Do they need forensics? Photographers? Detectives? How many people do they need to carry the body out? Once the police have a better picture of the situation, they will tell you to stay put and be on their way.

The Fujiyoshida police station is located to the southeast of Lake Kawaguchi. It can take about 20 or 30 minutes before they arrive in Aokigahara. Again they will take your information and ask simple questions. What are you doing in the forest? How did you find the body? You know you're not supposed to leave the track, right? Once they've gathered this information, they will ask you to take them to the body. Return to the suzuran tape and inform them that it leads to the corpse. Depending on the officers, they may or may not ask you to go with them. Either way, leave the tape for the officers to dispose of. It will also be their only way out once they are done with the body, so if you join them and then take the tape with you as you leave, you'll be leaving them stranded in the forest. Even the police get lost without help!

Calling the police to alert them of a body can be a trying ordeal. For many visitors, it may be tempting to ignore it and move on. Someone else will no doubt find the body and report it instead. Let's just leave it to them. Alerting the police means waiting around, answering all sorts of questions, and then guiding officers deep into the forest in a process that can take several hours, if not an entire day. No-one can force you to call the police if you're exploring the forest and stumble across a body. Finding a body can be shocking enough, let alone the hours of legal process that follows. It's up to each person to make a choice for themselves what to do in a situation like this. Would you be happy knowing that you left a body behind just to avoid a few hours of dealing with police? That's for you to decide.

The process can be sped up slightly by directly calling the Fujiyoshida Police Station instead. This cuts out the waiting time while your information is transferred to them and then waiting for someone who's free to call you back. The Fujiyoshida officers are the ones who deal with the forest directly every single day. And, as you might expect, there are those amongst the force who also find Aokigahara exhausting to deal with. Writer Kurihara Toru mentions in his book *Jukai no Arukikata* that most of the officers he dealt with in the forest were friendly and understanding, but others were more worn down by the constant corpses they had to deal with. Removing the bodies (or their remains, whatever state of decay they may be in), investigating who they belong to, searching for living family members and informing them of a loved one's death, as well as the general physical nature of getting in and out of the forest all the time weighs heavily on some. It's a difficult job to do, and it never has a happy ending.

10. REMOVING THE BODIES

SO, WHAT HAPPENS once the police are done with their initial investigation and it's time to remove the body? Murata mentions in his book *Jukai Ko* that he once discovered a body late in the afternoon. Judging by the condition of it, the person had died not too long beforehand. The police came in and, seeing the body, told everybody that they would look after it, but first it was time to go home. Themselves included. Surprised that they would leave a body there, Murata asked why, only to be told that it would be dark soon, and thus too dangerous to remove it. They had to think about their own safety, after all. They would return in the morning to collect it. It was, after all, not going anywhere.

Removing a body from Aokigahara can be a timely process, and a dangerous one to boot. Depending on the state and location of the body, removal can be done by a single officer or may rely on a team with various equipment. In general, however, corpse removal is handled in one of two ways:

1. Skeletal remains are handled by two or three officers. The bones and any personal effects are split up into different vinyl bags and carried out of the forest. These bags are usually doubled so they don't break, but in the case of a particularly heavy bag of bones, a heavy-duty bag made of much sturdier material may be used instead. A full human skeleton can weigh anywhere from 10 to 15 kg, so

this can easily be handled by a single officer or two.

2. Bodies are handled by up to eight officers. The corpse will be wrapped or placed in a body bag and carried out on a stretcher. The stretcher has slings attached to each corner that the officers can wear to make travel over uneven ground easier. Once they reach flat ground, the body is then placed in a hand-drawn cart and wheeled back to the patrol car.

Bodies start to decompose almost immediately after death. Depending on the environment, this can slow or speed the process up, and Aokigahara is no different. In summer, a body can turn to bones within a single month thanks to the humidity and animals. In winter, the forest gets below freezing, so the rate of decomposition slows. It's not until spring rolls around that the process begins again, and by summer, there's a good chance that the body has again been reduced to nothing but bones.

It's not uncommon to find skeletal remains throughout the forest, but that doesn't necessarily mean they've been there a long time. That person could have been alive just a few months earlier. Outside of winter, a body that shows only minimal signs of decay means that the person passed away only recently. Possibly within the last few days, or even hours.

Once returned to the station, police will investigate whether a death is suspicious or not. This can be extremely difficult depending on the state of the corpse or bones, but is undertaken regardless. If any personal effects are discovered with the body, these are searched as the police attempt to identify the remains. If they are able to find identification, the family is informed and they will be asked to pick up the remains. The majority of bodies, however, do not carry ID. They don't wish to be discovered, after all. In this case, the police will post the time of discovery, sex, any distinguishing features, and personal effects on the Fujiyoshida homepage. If anyone has any information, then they can call the station.

These unclaimed bodies are then cremated at the local government's expense and the ashes sent to local temples. The mausoleum in Narusawa Village was rebuilt in the 1990s so that it could hold the great number of unclaimed ashes it received. Cremation can cost as much as 100,000 yen, depending on the state of the body, all of which comes out of the local government's pockets. This can add up to millions of yen a year dealing with the remains of unknown and unclaimed bodies. People may go to the forest so that they don't burden their family with heavy funeral costs, but someone has to pay, and in the majority of cases, it's the people of Narusawa.

11. SUICIDE PREVENTION

NUMEROUS METHODS HAVE been undertaken over the years to prevent people from committing suicide inside Aokigahara. As soon as it became evident that the forest had become a suicide spot, the local government began implementing measures to remind people that other options were available to them, and things didn't have to end this way.

One of the first measures taken was the implementation of signs around the forest urging people to reconsider if they were thinking about suicide. One such sign says, "Your life is a precious gift from your parents. Quietly consider your parents, your siblings, and your children once more. You don't need to suffer alone, talk things over with us first." This sign, measuring 2 metres high by 1.2 metres wide, is perhaps the most well-known of all the suicide prevention signs because it's located at the entrance to the forest. This is followed by a number people can call for help.

On July 25, 2007, another sign went up that states, "We can settle your debt! We were saved as well!" This phone number connects people with an organisation made up of former debt victims who can help people get back on their feet and get loan sharks off their back; one of the biggest reasons why people decide to commit suicide in the forest. It's unknown how many lives have been saved by these signs, but the people on the other end have received numerous calls from those contemplating suicide, and have talked many of them out of it.

You can also find numerous suicide prevention

yobikake, or invitation, boxes around the forest. At 50 centimetres high and 30 centimetres wide, these white wooden boxes have a clear plastic front so people can see the leaflets inside. They're tied to trees at eye level so they stand out and located around the entrances, hiking trails, and other popular areas. These leaflets are another attempt to dissuade people from suicide by reminding them of the pain their family and friends will feel at their loss, and they sometimes include pictures of corpses found in the forest. It's hoped that these gruesome sights will make people turn away.

Perhaps realising that these passive efforts weren't having as big of an effect as they hoped, in 2008, the government turned to suicide prevention volunteers. As their name suggests, these volunteers (also referred to as "gatekeepers") are usually locals who patrol the popular tourist areas, particularly the car parks leading into Aokigahara; the final stops most people make before going in.

These volunteers are trained to look for telltale signs, such as being alone, carrying little to no extraneous items, looking around listlessly, wearing clothes unsuited to hiking (such as a business suit), and arriving by public transport. If someone fits the profile and appears to be depressed, the volunteers will approach and speak to them, asking them how they are, why they're at the forest, and if they need help. If they suspect a person of being suicidal, they will stay with them until the police or medical services arrive, and are known to be persistent in this goal. So persistent that many people have called them out over the years for being overbearing and pushy, even detaining people who had no intention of committing suicide at all. They just "looked the type." While their hearts may be in the right place, the suicide prevention volunteers have been known to be overzealous at times. Perhaps in a case of "better safe than sorry."

The Yamanashi Prefecture "Aokigahara Suicide Countermeasures Project" states:

"In order to decrease the number of suicides taking place in our prefecture, measures are necessary to stop people coming from outside to commit suicide here, along with suicide prevention measures for prefectural citizens as well. In particular, measures are necessary to stop people from coming to Aokigahara from outside the prefecture to commit suicide."

It's somewhat dense, but the official line is that Yamanashi Prefecture sees abnormally high suicide rates because of Aokigahara Forest, and they want people to stop coming from outside the prefecture to do it. They are the ones left to deal with it, after all. With volunteers working under these guidelines, it's easy to see why they can appear overzealous with stopping people to talk, especially if they're entering Aokigahara on public transport. Aokigahara regulars recommend carrying a camera and wearing clothes suitable for hiking if you don't wish to be constantly stopped by them. They're looking for people who *aren't* there for hiking, after all.

In recent years, the manager of Narusawa Ice

Cave, Watanabe Kyoji, has taken to plugging his speakers in and playing guitar deep into the night in his own prevention efforts. This all began when he was playing guitar at home one night and a young woman stopped to listen. She was planning on entering the forest to kill herself, but the sound of the guitar stirred something inside her and she couldn't go through with it.

Realising the potential power behind music, Watanabe took to playing each night in the hopes of preventing more deaths. Even if he couldn't see them, even if it was only in his immediate area, even if it only affected one single person, then it would be worth it. Believing that music has a way of reaching people through their pain, Watanabe continues his playing each night, reminding people that they are not alone, and that someone else is out there with them.

12. POPULARITY OVERSEAS

THANKS TO *NAMI no Tou* and its growing popularity as a suicide spot, Aokigahara is a name few in Japan would never have heard of. It's not only well-known within Japan, however, and its renown has been growing internationally in recent years as well. A quick type of "Aokigahara" into an English search engine will bring back countless pages of the "terrifying and mysterious suicide forest of Japan." How to get there, what to do there, top 10 lists of the most terrifying things about it, and so on. Sometimes it feels like the overseas media are far more interested in the forest than Japan itself is.

In his book *Jukai Ko*, Murata Ramu mentions that he received an email from a popular entertainment company in Japan one day. That email requested his help in showing Clown, a musician from the American metal group Slipknot, around Aokigahara. Clown was visiting Japan for promotions and mentioned that he really wanted to visit the infamous suicide forest. They walked around for several hours, taking photos and looking around, before finally visiting a shrine to be cleansed. Part of his Japanese promotional company's conditions for allowing Clown to visit the forest apparently involved everyone being purified before leaving. Murata, who by his own words doesn't believe in ghosts or gods, remarked he had no idea how Clown felt about the idea, but in the end everyone returned home safely, so what harm was there in it? It was another tiny piece of Japanese culture for him to take home.

In 2015, *The Sea of Trees* was released, starring Matthew McConaughey, Naomi Watts, and Ken Watanabe. In it, an American man and a Japanese man attempt to take their lives in the eponymous forest, but both find themselves struggling to go through with it, and through flashbacks their troubles are revealed. The film went by the name *Tsuioku no Mori* in Japanese, or The Forest of Reminiscence, which better summed up the content of the film for an audience already well aware of the Sea of Trees.

The majority of the movie was filmed in the United States, however, and it shows; the forest in the film looks nothing like Aokigahara's famous unlevel ground, twisting roots, and moss-covered trees. Yet, the fact that it was even made to begin with was a testament to how popular Aokigahara was becoming overseas. It was known worldwide as a suicide spot. The main character in the film was suicidal. This, for some reason, makes him want to travel all the way to Japan so he can end his life in the infamous suicide forest. The film was, perhaps unsurprisingly, not well received, but it also wouldn't be the last foreign production based in the Sea of Trees.

The following year, *The Forest* was released. This film instead chose to go by *Jukai* in Japan, a more suitable name for a movie more squarely placed in the horror genre. Unlike the slow, unfolding character drama of *The Sea of Trees*, *The Forest* decided to go for the "terrifying suicide forest" route and throws all sorts of ghosts and creepy legends at its main character, who enters the forest looking for her missing sister. Needless to say, this film wasn't very well received either.

Producer David S. Goyer reportedly came up for the idea of the film after reading about Aokigahara on Wikipedia, becoming "obsessed with it," and deciding that it would make a fantastic location for a horror film. Filming for this movie's forest took place in Serbia; in general, the Japanese government doesn't allow films or large-scale film-making to take place inside the forest, so there is little way to avoid this. It resulted in yet another un-Aokigahara-like forest, however, and neither critics nor viewers have been kind to the plot. Japanese viewers were also quick to point out that there are no such things as the Aokigahara Station or Narusawa Information Desk presented in the movie, among a slew of other false information presented about the forest and even Mount Fuji itself (it was, apparently, researched from Wikipedia after all...).

Overseas tourism to Aokigahara has been on the rise over the years. A lot of this is thanks to unsavoury media attention, a sudden emergence of films and documentaries in the English language, and also simple curiosity. This isn't to say that Aokigahara isn't presented as a "scary suicide forest" within Japan itself; it is. This seems to be magnified tenfold overseas, however, and locals have reported foreigners asking them "where they can see the dead bodies."

Aokigahara has long been an area of beauty, folklore, and rich history to its locals. International visitors have none of this history with the forest, and may know nothing about it other than "lots of people die there and you can sometimes come across the bodies."

The language barrier also plays a large part in this. While there is ample information available about Aokigahara in Japanese, there's not a lot in English, and sometimes, what information gets through can even be falsified. Murata, the same writer who took Clown on a tour of the forest and is considered by many to be an expert, admitted to doing so himself.

In an interview with an American magazine called "Girls & Corpses," the magazine asked him why Japanese people choose to die in the forest. "The goddess Konohanasakuya-hime, one of the ancestors of our Imperial family, is worshipped there. We Japanese choose to die there so we can be closer to the gods."

If you've come this far, you should know that's a blatant lie, and Murata even said he deliberately lied when answering. Why? Simply because he wanted the lie to spread. Perhaps he was sick of constantly being asked, or perhaps he wasn't fond of the magazine's approach to the forest. Either way, false information can easily be presented to an international audience that doesn't speak Japanese, and it's much more difficult for them to confirm or deny without access to the same resources the Japanese have.

Through the Japanese government's efforts, Aokigahara's fame as a suicide spot had been waning in recent years. Reportedly, less people have been committing suicide in the forest, and the government's focus on the forest as a place of beauty, as a tourist attraction where you can see beautiful scenery that you can't get anywhere else is slowly helping to change its image. Much of that work was undone thanks to international media attention over the last few years, however, and again Aokigahara has been thrust back in the spotlight as a suicide forest. Only this time, the world over.

One local who spoke with the *Global Times* newspaper reportedly said, "The first wave of notoriety was created by mass media decades ago, and now we are facing a second wave created by social media. Now that it's recognised globally, people are coming from all over the world... to see something unusual."

This international attention in recent years seems to have reset much of the progress the Japanese government had been making with regards to turning around the forest's dark image. This, combined with the ease of sharing information on the internet and the popularity of clickbait titles and top ten lists has once more sparked a "suicide forest" revival, and not one that's welcome for those who are trying to protect the forest's heritage.

DEMYSTIFYING THE LEGENDS

AOKIGAHARA IS REGARDED BY MANY as a place of mystery. You go in, get lost, and never come out again. It's a dark, scary maze where everything looks the same and its only purpose is to swallow you alive. Who knows what truly happens inside the Sea of Trees. With a name like that, it can't be anything good, right? Its fame as a suicide spot has only increased that infamy over the years, and numerous stories, urban legends, and other nefarious rumours have sprung to life surrounding it. But do these stories have any truth to them, or are they just that? Stories made to spook and scare? Let's take a look at some and find out.

13. URBAN LEGENDS

THINK ABOUT THE stories you've heard of Aokigahara. What immediately comes to mind? Chances are good that you've heard about how if you enter the forest, you'll never leave it again. Maybe you've heard that compasses don't work due to the strong magnetic pull in the volcanic floor. Perhaps you've even heard that the yakuza use the forest as a secret dumping ground for those they kill. There are numerous urban legends surrounding the Aokigahara Sea of Trees, so let's take a look at the real truth behind them.

Compasses Don't Work

This is probably the most famous of all Aokigahara legends. If you enter the Sea of Trees with a compass, you can kiss your way out goodbye, because that compass isn't going to work for long. Once you enter the forest, compasses go crazy. They love that volcanic floor bed and will spin around and around thanks to their magnetic attraction. This myth has been spread for decades, both in and outside of Japan. Is there any truth to it? Will your compass actually go crazy once you step inside the forest?

The simple answer is: no.

Well, you might be thinking, that's disappointing. If it's not true, then how did such a rumour start to begin with? It's not like it's terribly difficult to prove or disprove. All you need to do is enter the forest yourself with a compass and you can check. If it's not true, why does the legend persist to this day?

This rumour is especially beloved because it plays on people's fears of the deep, dark forest that's out to get you however it can. Once you step off that populated walking track, you're in uncharted territory. The ground rises and falls, full of potholes, caves, and tunnels that are hidden beneath tree roots and green moss that snakes all over. Everything looks the same, no matter what direction you turn. You can be only 20 metres from the path and have no idea where you are, or which way to turn to get back to safety. What if, on top of that, your compass also didn't work? Well, that would be horrific! But it's also untrue.

Legends of crazy compasses began because the hardened magma floor of Aokigahara *does* contain iron ore and magnetite. Hearing this, many people assumed that this would influence compasses, but it's not that easy. Walking through the forest with a compass in hand will show no change, not even a slither of confusion. Well, maybe it's not spinning in crazy circles, but no doubt the needle is pointing in the wrong direction, right? Again, you can confirm this yourself with GPS. Compasses work just fine in Aokigahara, and they continue to point in the direction they're supposed to, as GPS will confirm.

Okay, well, there has to be some area in the forest where the compasses go crazy? You're just not standing in the right spot! Again, no. Nobody has ever found an area of the forest where compasses don't work exactly as they're supposed to. As much as people want this legend to be true, it just isn't. Now, if you place your compass directly on the forest floor, it's true that the needle might wobble a bit... but that's all. It still points north, albeit with a slight stutter thanks to the iron in the rocks, and sometimes it doesn't even do that. It's also safe to assume that most people will be walking with their compass held somewhere around chest height, not crawling as they drag their compass along the ground.

Compasses work just fine.

If You Enter, You'll Never Leave Again

Alongside the popular "compasses don't work," this is likely the other most famous tale told about Aokigahara. Once you leave the walking paths and enter the forest, that's it. You'll never get out again. By now you should realise how silly that rumour is. Plenty of people go in and out of the forest all the time. Even if we exclude the popular tourist areas, the internet era has seen countless people come and go from Aokigahara with no problem whatsoever. You can watch them on the internet right now.

This is a holdover from long ago, when it was dangerous to enter the forest unassisted. These days, people know that if they plan to go exploring, they need to be prepared. Whether that means a compass, GPS, suzuran tape, or whatever method you plan to use, if you're not prepared then yes, chances are good that you'll get lost and potentially never find your way out again. But that's not guaranteed. If you prepare yourself, it's actually very difficult to get lost.

Suzuran tape, or just plain marking tape, is a simple, old-school way to find your way out. Tie one end of the colourful tape to a tree, unroll it as you explore, and then follow it back when you're ready to leave. In the past, people also left bright neon tape on trees as they walked, kind of like a trail of breadcrumbs, but more visible. It's not recommended that you do this now, because it litters the forest and isn't very reliable if you forget where you placed the tape, but it wasn't uncommon not that long ago. Other people used to spray paint trees, either marking them with an X or leaving a number. Again, it's not very common now, but you can still find trees in the forest that have this paint on them. The easiest and most failsafe way to get around, however, is with a compass or GPS. You can explore to your heart's content and know exactly where you are at all times.

Be prepared, know what you are doing, and it's very difficult to get lost.

Cell Phones Don't Work

If you enter Aokigahara and get lost, don't expect to rely on your cell phone to get out; cell phones don't work. There's zero coverage in the Sea of Trees, or so the legends would have you believe.

This one is actually right on the money... for the most part. Aokigahara is massive and dense, and there are few reception towers around. Very few areas of the forest have any reception at all, and those tend to be close to the outskirts, near the national highway. "But the area is full of tourists! How can there not be any reception?" There is reception for tourists. In the tourist areas. Once you enter the forest, however, it's safer to assume that you're not going to be able to use your phone. You might find a patch here and there on the walking paths, but once you leave those, your phone is nothing more than an expensive portable game machine… if it can even play those offline.

There have been reports on the internet of people claiming that their cell phones worked just fine outside the tourist areas. They even displayed several reception bars, so clearly this rumour was a lie. The truth is, even if your phone displays reception bars, it doesn't mean that your call will get through. In fact, even if you do talk to someone inside the forest, and you can hear their voice, there's a good chance they won't be able to hear you at all. This is because of the antennas. The antennas servicing the area sit roughly 10 metres above ground, so they're sending their signal down to you from a high position, and they have a lot of power to do so. However, the tiny little phone in your hands, close to the ground and shielded beneath a dense canopy of trees, doesn't have that same power. The signal can't reach the antenna. You might be able to hear them, but they won't be able to hear you.

If you have a sudden need to use your phone inside Aokigahara (for example, if you find a body), then your best bet is to head towards the highway or one of the tourist car parks and use your phone from there. Inside the forest, it's just a dead weight.

Suicide Village

Perhaps "Suicide Village" isn't the best name for it, but one urban legend states that there is a village deep within Aokigahara where those who couldn't go through with committing suicide ended up forming their own society. There, hidden away from the rest of the world, they live a simple, peaceful lifestyle reminiscent of the old days. No technology, no jobs, no debt. People work and live for themselves away from the ever-watchful eye of "the man."

Sounds kind of nice, doesn't it? Who wouldn't want to get away from it all and start anew where nobody cares who you are or what your life on the outside was like? Where your only worry is looking after yourself and perhaps filling any free time you might have. No taxes, no deadlines, no boss breathing down your neck, and nobody berating you over how much of a failure you are. It makes sense, right? Not everybody who enters Aokigahara to kill themselves can actually go through with it, and it's a big place. A lot of people set up tents to spend the night or a few days before they finally commit the deed. What if those people somehow found each other and started their own community away from the world?

There is, however, no such village. In this day and age of drones and constant aerial surveillance, you would think such a village would be picked up from the air. Even the smallest gap in the trees would betray a village beneath their branches, not to mention how much space people would have to carve out to produce land for farming. If you're going to cut yourself off from the world, you need to eat somehow, and that involves growing your own food.

As you can no doubt guess, Aokigahara isn't exactly the best place to farm. People have, in fact, tried to make the area habitable in the past. They were unsuccessful. Even if we suppose that these people don't grow farm food, but instead live as carnivores, there's not exactly a wealth of animals to feed on. Animals do live in the forest, yes, even large animals like bears and deer. But it's rare to come across them, and hunting across such treacherous terrain is more likely to leave the hunter injured than the prey.

There *is* a village within Aokigahara, although it's not quite the village that people might expect from this tall tale. If you look at a map of Aokigahara from above, you'll see it beneath Lake Shouji. It's called Lake Shouji Inn Village, because like its name states, it's a village full of travellers inns. Rumours on the internet have claimed that this village was the infamous "Suicide Village," or even that it's a secret government facility hidden in the trees. Considering that it's right there on the map and anyone can walk around, enjoy some nice food in lovely restaurants, and spend the night in one of the many comfortable inns... that's highly unlikely. The village has its own grocery store, hairdresser, post office, and even a (now abandoned) elementary school!

If you're looking for a juicy legend, this one isn't it. There is no village hidden within Aokigahara's depths of those who have shunned the outside world. It does make for a good story though!

Gangs of Wild Dogs

You're taking a stroll through the forest. It's a beautiful, calm day, so you decide to explore a little further in. You don't plan on going too far, and you have some tape to safely guide you back. What could go wrong?

Before long you hear a noise in the distance. It sounds like growling. Could it be a bear? You've heard they live in the forest, although few people have ever run into one. As you get closer, you realise it's not a bear. It's a dog. Phew. You reach out to pat it, but it hunkers down and growls even louder. How did it even get here? You soon realise that the dog isn't alone, though. Not even close. Members of its pack emerge from behind the trees, and judging by the look of them, they only have one thing on their mind. These dogs have a taste for flesh, and you're next.

If you believe the rumours, packs of wild dogs roam Aokigahara forest feeding upon the flesh of the dead. This sustains them, and they have a taste for it. If you're unlucky enough to stumble upon them yourself, then your chances of escaping unscathed are horribly low. Leaflets from the Fujiyoshida police even once stated that "most bodies found in Aokigahara are nothing more than bones or heavily decomposed, eaten away by wild birds and dogs." If the police are saying it, then surely it must be true? Just like the infamous

Suicide Village, however, this legend is also false. Or at least, nobody's ever found any proof of it.

First and foremost, dogs have never been sighted inside Aokigahara. Just as the forest isn't exactly inviting or even habitable for humans, it's not very convenient for dogs either, let alone packs of them. There's little food, and even if we suppose that the dogs are living off the flesh of the dead, there aren't enough people committing suicide to sustain a whole pack, let alone several.

A few dogs are known to hang around the car parks of touristy areas, but they get more than enough food there and are otherwise quite friendly. Some people also claim to have heard the barks of dogs inside the forest, but others attribute those sounds to birds instead. Besides, if they were wild dogs on the hunt, they probably wouldn't bark to give away their position in the first place…

It's thought this rumour surfaced because animals *do* eat the flesh of those who have committed suicide inside the Sea of Trees. They're just not wild dogs. It's not uncommon for someone to come across a body where the flesh has been eaten and dung found nearby. The immediate conclusion most would jump to is that of a dog or a bear (rumours of flesh eating bears also exist).

All sorts of tiny animals live in the forest that consume flesh, not to mention the mass of insects that make their home in a body after death. Writer and frequent explorer of Aokigahara, Kurihara Toru, set up an experiment to see if wild dogs really did roam the forest. He bought some chicken on the bone from the supermarket and set up a video to record what happened overnight. In the morning, much of the meat was gone. It was revealed to be the work not of dogs, however, but a tiny field mouse. What the mouse didn't eat was then swarmed by giant ants.

As gruesome as it sounds, sometimes the lower half of a body can be found separated from the upper half, still swinging in the trees. It's not strange to wonder if an animal tugging at the legs is the cause, but often it's not an animal at all. As the body decays, it's not unusual for the lower torso to rot and fall off the body thanks to gravity. No animals needed.

But what about bears? If it's not dogs, then surely it could be the work of a bear? Some people swear by the fact that bears exist in Aokigahara. It has never 100% been proven, but it's never been disproven, either. Is there a bear in the forest? Perhaps several? Maybe. It's a big place, and humans only touch a small part of it on a daily basis. Some locals warn explorers to wear bells or keep a radio playing to warn the animals away. Better to be safe than sorry, after all. But wild packs of rabid dogs? They don't exist. Even for them, Aokigahara isn't very sustainable living.

Homicidal Lurkers

This legend makes the rounds on the internet with surprising regularity. Word has it that homicidal maniacs lurk in Aokigahara's depths, waiting for new victims to claim. It's the perfect crime, isn't it? A treacherous, near-impenetrable forest that most are scared to enter. Just a few metres off the track and you'll find yourself in an environment where everything looks the same. It's dark, oppressive, and nothing but moss-covered ground and the same rotting trees everywhere you look. There's no telling which way you came from, or which way is back. If you get lost, it'll take a long time for a search team to mobilise and start looking for you. Plenty of time for someone to make you actually disappear... for good.

Not to mention the large number of people who visit Aokigahara to end their own lives. These people, supposedly, are the homicidal maniacs' most favoured targets. After all, they came here to kill themselves in the first place. That generally means they'll have wrapped everything up back in their home life before they set out. Many people who have made the decision to commit suicide will first make sure to tie up all loose ends. They'll cancel phone contracts. Close bank accounts. End rental contracts. In doing so, authorities won't need to chase them up for late payments, or search for their whereabouts. They don't want to be found, so making sure everything is settled first is a good way to disappear from the world.

The perfect crime.

Scenes like this have featured in horror media before. Usually delivered with a line like, "You wanted to kill yourself, right? Well, I'll do it for you!" After all, who is going to be able to tell the difference between a murder and a suicide in a forest popularly known as "The Suicide Forest"? A murder committed in summer could see the body turn to bones within a few short weeks. By that point, there's likely to be little evidence left suggesting that this could be anything other than a suicide.

But is it true? Do murderers really lurk in the forest, sating their bloodlust on those unfortunate enough to cross their path? The answer is... probably not. But, there is a chance.

Just like with rumours of the bears, it's impossible to say that people like this don't visit Aokigahara. The rumours don't suggest these people live in the forest, they just visit it for fun. They could be regular, every day folk who visit in their free time to indulge in their deepest, darkest fantasies.

Bodies have been found that showed signs of injuries after death, and even bodies that were burnt. Bodies decay so fast and are often ravaged by animals so quickly that it's near impossible to tell. The police do investigate every body they come across in the forest, even those that are nothing more than skeletal remains, but often it's difficult to tell exactly what happened. How can you confirm a person was strangled to death if all you have left are their bones? How can you tell that a person was stabbed if animals have already eaten most of their flesh and scraped at the bones?

This is a legend that can't really be proven one way or the other. At best, it's highly unlikely. It's a lot of work for someone to go in the hopes that they'll just happen across someone out of view from the public. Even if they patrol the common suicide zone, it's still a massive area and requires a lot of luck to cross someone's path at the right time. But it's not impossible, and if everything lines up right, it really is the perfect crime. To a homicidal maniac, that might be worth the time and effort put in.

Most who are familiar with Aokigahara agree that this one is a bit of a stretch, but it's also hard to say with 100% certainty that it has never, ever happened before.

Yakuza Dumping Ground

Legend has it that the yakuza use Aokigahara as their own personal dumping ground. Similar to the homicidal murderers who claim suicide victims because no-one will ever be able to tell the difference, the yakuza dump bodies inside the forest so nobody will ever know it was them. They force their victims to write a suicide note first, kill them elsewhere, and then dump the bodies in the forest. They carry them in late at night, when nobody's around, and it doubles as a test of courage. And if the bodies are ever found, well, the suicide note that accompanies them is the perfect cover story.

You can find comments from people all over the internet claiming to have seen gang members carrying large bags into the forest before disappearing; bags large enough to fit a human body. Could a gang member really dispose of a body in such treacherous terrain and then get out alive themselves? How much truth is there to this one?

As it turns out, there is at least some. Writer Murata Ramu, who is well known for his coverage of Aokigahara and the many books and articles he has written over the years, ventured into the forest with a known gang member at the request of a magazine he was working for. Working under the title of "Returning to the Scene of the Crime with the Criminal!", Murata entered Aokigahara with the man in question late at night. It turned out that the gang member had not dumped a body in the forest, but actually murdered him there and *then* left the body. That was the story the magazine wanted to cover.

The gang member informed them that the man he murdered had tried to kill him first. He was encroaching on his territory. When the man was unable to kill him, however, the gang member turned the tables and attacked him instead. He was no stranger to murder, but this would be the one that got him locked up, and for one ironic reason: dumping the body inside Aokigahara.

According to the gang member, he didn't dump the body in Aokigahara to hide it. On the contrary, he wanted it found. He figured news would get out of the man's "suicide" and this would demonstrate to his rivals and subordinates that he wasn't to be messed with, but in the end, it just got him arrested.

The gang member, his subordinate, and the victim entered the forest through the Lake Sai Bat Cave parking lot. At this point, the victim was still alive because they figured carrying him into the forest would be a hassle. They made the man walk himself, and then finally killed him inside, forcibly hanging him. It's no easy feat to walk through the forest at night, as even torches do little to light the way, but they managed to make their way a respectable distance inside and get back out again.

The body was eventually found, the police suspected foul play, and the gang member was arrested. Murata asked him if there was anything he was scared of, considering the lengths he went to in order to kill the man. "Ghosts," he replied, trembling as he pointed out there was one walking next to them at that exact moment. He was, according to Murata, entirely serious, and the thing that he found scariest of all.

It's impossible to say whether this is a common occurrence. It's unlikely, however, because of the difficulty in entering and leaving the forest, particularly at night, and even more so if you're carrying a body at the same time. This is the same reason the above-mentioned gang member made his victim walk. Can we say with 100% certainty that it has never happened? Of course not. The above story proves that to be untrue. But is it as common as this urban legend would have you believe? Probably not. There are easier ways for the yakuza to get rid of a body that doesn't involve going all the way to Aokigahara, a hefty distance to travel for most yakuza gangs.

As an interesting aside, variations of this legend have developed in recent years claiming that the yakuza are working hand-in-hand with certain corporations who dump industrial waste in the forest. The yakuza throw their dead bodies into the mix, pay the corporation some big money, and it all gets dumped together inside the forest. There is, of course, no evidence of either the mass dumping of waste nor corpses hidden inside it. By now you can probably imagine how difficult that would be to begin with, making this particular variation a colourful flight of fancy.

Supernatural Lurkers

Perhaps unsurprisingly for a forest popularly known as the Suicide Forest, Aokigahara is rife with urban legends that speak of supernatural entities haunting the trees. There are all sorts of tales; if you can think of it, someone's probably already told it. Ghostly voices call out from the trees. Photos taken in the forest reveal spirits when developed. Spirits lure you purposefully to your doom. The list goes on.

One of the more famous legends tells the tale of the woman in the red dress. She appears before people who have entered the forest looking to kill themselves, admonishing them for their choice. Once they change their mind and decide to leave, she suddenly disappears. It's believed that she's the spirit of someone who committed suicide long ago, and she doesn't want others to make the same mistake as her.

Other versions of the story have her spending time with people who find themselves lost in the forest. She waits with them until the search teams arrive, and when everyone is safely back, suddenly the person will notice she's gone. "Where is the woman in the red dress who was with me? Is she okay?" At this point the search team will reveal that nobody saw this supposed woman in the red dress.

Was she real, or...? This story is so famous that there's even an adult video based on it...

Another legend states that there's a ghostly monk in the woods who reads Buddhist sutras. His voice carries on the wind, although it's difficult to tell which direction it's coming from. He continues praying for the dead, even though he is one himself... This one can easily be explained by the nearby highways. The sound of cars driving, backfiring, and even the exhaust of modded bikes that roam the area can travel unexpectedly far. Depending on the strength of the wind and the direction it's blowing, the sounds can grow louder or smaller, almost imitating the sound of a human voice chanting. It's not a monk. Just some nearby cars.

What about the mysterious woman's laugh that people hear deep in the trees? There's no mistaking someone's laughter for the sound of a car's exhaust, is there? Surely that's a positive sign that the forest is haunted? Well, not really, because this one is also easily explained.

A great majority of visitors to Aokigahara enter through the same place; Fugaku Wind Cave or Narusawa Ice Cave. Most people who decide to explore the forest leave the track near these areas, and as we've explained elsewhere, trekking through the forest is no easy feat. While you may think you've gone quite a distance, at least a few hundred metres, in reality you've probably only gone close to 50. Up and down over valleys and hills, around potholes and caves, through and around mossy roots and never once finding any even ground to make good time; people rarely make it too far from the tracks, even though they might feel like they have. That woman's laughter? Most researchers agree it's just tourists on the walking paths, the wind carrying their laughter in.

Okay, but how about the ghost photos? Legend has it that if you take a photo inside Aokigahara, you'll have a good chance of capturing a spirit on film. If you have facial recognition on, the camera will find faces where no faces actually exist... This, surely, is proof.

As in many other countries, ghost photos are all the rage in Japan. Not just in Aokigahara, but photos taken in well-known haunted locations all around the country purport to have captured spirits on film. Within Aokigahara, many of these can be explained simply by the scenery. There are a lot of things that look like faces in the forest, and it's not hard for a camera to recognise these as eyes, nose, and a mouth. Twisted roots grown in the shape of a face, piles of leaves covering moss and rubbish, shadows, light, dips and curves; you don't have to look hard to find something in the vicinity that resembles a human face, and when captured on film, chances are it looks even more ghastly.

Phantom Paths

When you look at an official map of Aokigahara Forest, you'll notice only a few designated paths are marked. There are, however, other paths hidden within the forest. Paths you won't find on any map. What were they for, and why were they erased from the maps?

Look at any map and you'll see the main paths. These tend to be concentrated in the tourist areas, with a few more here and there cutting through the forest. If you believe the rumours, however, there are even more phantom paths hidden that don't show up on any map. Paths that, for some reason or another, were erased from history. Perhaps they were too dangerous. Perhaps they simply fell out of use. Perhaps someone is trying to hide what's at the other end, and they no longer want the public to be able to find what lurks deep beyond the trees.

As with any good urban legend, what was an otherwise mundane tale has been given a sinister twist, and now exists as a mysterious phantom path hidden within the Suicide Forest. Does it lead to the Suicide Village? Does it carry you to your doom? Does it appear only to lure you further in and then disappear so you'll never find your way out? Where does it exist, and how are we supposed to find it?

There *are* old paths all throughout Aokigahara. This is not in dispute. Many fall out of use and trees grow back over them. The forest is in a constant state of decay and rebirth, so it doesn't take long for a little-used path to simply disappear. You can generally tell the location of an old path because the ground may be more flat than its surroundings, or it may appear as a valley with "walls" on either side, even if it's now overgrown with trees. You may also find stone or wooden signs that remain where a path once diverged, now rotting or covered in moss themselves. Sometimes these paths can appear so wide that a car could easily drive through and disappear into the darkness. How were they made? What really lies at the end?

In most cases, they're just walking paths that fell out of use. Some other paths, however, have a much longer history. No, they don't lead to long-lost hidden villages, nor were they designed to lead travellers astray. Some paths were simply used to cart ice.

Before refrigerators became common, ice was regularly farmed from the caves in Aokigahara. During the Meiji era, large paths were constructed to allow horse-drawn carts to carry this ice out and ship it off to where it needed to go. As technology progressed and ice was no longer necessary, nobody needed to use the paths anymore. Nature grew back, and now they have become phantom paths; not immediately visible upon first glance, but the longer you look at them, the stranger they seem.

These phantom paths aren't out to get you. They don't lead anywhere dark and mysterious. They're just old and no longer in use, another victim of the passage of time.

Phantom Lake

There are five famous lakes that surround Mount Fuji, but did you know that there is another? Legend has it that a mysterious phantom lake exists within the Sea of Trees. It appears and disappears like a mirage in the forest, baffling all who happen to come across it. Even more baffling is that the water is said to be red, like the colour of blood...

Only 20 metres from National Highway 139,

you'll find a small lake called Akaike, or Red Pond. Yes, it's a real lake, and like the legend states, it appears and disappears, showing up roughly once every 10 years. It's for this reason that some also call it the Phantom Lake. There's nothing supernatural about it, however. Akaike is very real, and there's a scientific reason for why it appears and disappears. It's believed to be connected to Lake Shoji through an underground tunnel, and it only appears when the waters of Lake Shoji rise. Calling it a lake may be generous, as it has a diameter of only 70 metres, but it can reach depths of close to 10 metres when full.

Until 50 years ago, Akaike was a permanent lake. Said to be connected underground to Lakes Shoji and Saiko, part of what used to be the single and much larger Senoumi, it now sits alone inside Aokigahara. In the past, the lake would freeze during winter and locals used it for ice skating. However, when several companies moved in and started using the lakes for hydroelectric power generation, the sixth lake of Mount Fuji began to slowly disappear. Now it only appears when there's an excess of water, and then shortly drains away again.

Akaike gets its name from the appearance of water in the area. When the area near Akaike floods, the earth becomes unable to hold it in and the water sits on top, turning reddish-brown. It's sadly not a blood lake in the middle of Aokigahara, as awesome as that legend might sound, but it does exist. At least, once every 10 years or so, anyway.

Corpses Everywhere

This is a legend that is perhaps more prevalent overseas than it is within Japan, but there are Japanese people who believe it as well. The image of Aokigahara as a suicide forest is so strong that some believe it is littered with corpses. As in, everywhere. You can't turn a corner without running into one. If you leave the main path, you'll immediately trip over some bones, or perhaps find yourself face-to-face with a body hanging from a tree. The forest is nothing but trees and bones, or so they'd have you believe.

If you've come this far, you should already know how silly this one is. This myth is generally perpetuated by people who have never been to the forest before, and the only information they're relying on is "this many people died in the forest during this particular year!" You hear a lot about when somebody finds a body, but you don't hear about the other 200 times they went exploring and found nothing. Murata Ramu, a writer who has been exploring Aokigahara for several decades, claims that he's seen perhaps 20 bodies in total. Most of them were nothing but bones. That might seem like a large number, but this is over hundreds of visits over decades of years, and often with people whose sole purpose is to explore the forest to find a body. It's not unusual for journalists to want to write a piece about Aokigahara, explore the forest with a guide so they can gather evidence first-hand, and return home with nothing. Several times in a row.

There are bodies in the forest, yes. They are not

lying everywhere, no. They are generally quite difficult to find.

Secret Cults

Did you know that there are numerous religious cults hiding deep within Aokigahara? Somewhere, deep in the trees, secret cults have taken root and they practice dark traditions that must remain hidden from the outside world. Only within Aokigahara can they thrive, away from the public eye and free to do as they wish. That's what the legends would have you believe, anyway.

Mount Fuji has long been worshipped as a sacred mountain. It is a *goshintai*, or physical embodiment of a *kami*. It's not just a mountain. It's a god. The kami enshrined at Mount Fuji is none other than Konohanasakuya-hime, also known in shortened form as Sakuya-hime (the blossom princess). She is the wife of Ninigi, the grandson of Amaterasu who was sent to earth and eventually fathered what would become the line of emperors that still preside over Japan today. Sakuya-hime's father originally proposed that Ninigi marry her older sister, Iwa-Naga-hime (the rock princess) instead, but Ninigi found her appearance loathsome and insisted upon the beautiful blossom princess. For this reason, it's said that human lives are short, like that of a flower, instead of long-lasting, like that of a rock. Thanks, Ninigi.

But Sakuya-hime has a bit of a temper on her, and she became known as the goddess of volcanoes as well. Shrines all over Mount Fuji, the biggest and baddest volcano of all, are dedicated to her in the hopes of keeping it (and her) from erupting. Clearly something ticked her off in the 800s, however, and because of that we have Aokigahara today.

As such, Mount Fuji is no stranger to religion. It is one of the most important Shinto locations in all of Japan. But according to urban legends, it's not just Shinto that's worshipped at Mount Fuji anymore. Deep in the forest, you'll find all sorts of secret cults and religions. One in particular you may well be familiar with: Aum Shinrikyo.

Aum Shinrikyo were a doomsday cult led by Asahara Shoko in 1984. They carried out the Matsumoto sarin attack in 1994 and the Tokyo subway sarin attack in 1995. 20 people were killed across both attacks, and hundreds more injured. Asahara was eventually arrested and sentenced to death for organising the attacks, being executed on July 6, 2018. And the Aum Shinrikyo headquarters? At the foot of Mount Fuji, to the south of Aokigahara Forest. In this case, the urban legends are true. Or at least, they were. Aum Shinrikyo's presence in Aokigahara will be explored in further detail shortly, but after the Tokyo subway sarin attacks, their headquarters near Aokigahara were raided and torn down. Now you'll find a large public park in their place, with a single memorial stone placed in remembrance.

Believe it or not, Aum Shinrikyo aren't the only cult confirmed to have once resided in the area. Deep within Aokigahara is a building referred to as *Kentoku Dojo*. This roughly translates to "Emperor's Virtue Training Ground." There have long been rumours of a mysterious monk who resides within Aokigahara. Nobody was ever quite sure if he was real, a legend, and what exactly he was doing there in the first place. That monk was a real person, however, and he lived in Kentoku Dojo.

He lived there with his wife. When visited by writer Murata Ramu in the late 2000s, he claimed to be working on a "secret project." If information of that project reached the outside world, something terrible would happen, he claimed. He had been living there since the end of World War II. He entered the forest intending to kill himself, but instead stumbled across the area where Kentoku Dojo now stands. There, he found a cave with a stone monument before it. It was dedicated to the mountain religion of Mount Fuji. It was old. Extremely old. The monk claimed the building he constructed on that spot was to prepare people for the "coming of the gods." People would no longer be around once this happened, however. He was preparing for the end of humanity as we knew it.

The monk unfortunately hasn't been seen for close to a decade now. Whether he finally left Aokigahara, or something else happened to him, nobody knows. Perhaps he finally finished his secret project and moved on. Perhaps, in his advanced age, he passed away. Nobody knows, but Kentoku Dojo still stands strong in the middle of the forest, now abandoned.

Are there any other secret cults hiding in Aokigahara at present? Probably not. The area is well-explored and well-populated these days, but this is one case where the urban legends did have some truth behind them. Aum Shinrikyo orchestrated their most devastating attack from here, and the Kentoku Dojo has confounded and even terrified people for generations. But let's take a closer look at both.

14. RELIGION IN THE FOREST

IN 1828, A monk visited Shoji Village, claiming, "The hole is calling to me." That hole was what we now call Shoji no O-ana, a cave that sits just beyond Kentoku Dojo. At the time, it was referred to as Seiji no O-ana, and it was worshipped as a cave where one could be reborn. The monk's name was Seigyo, and he proclaimed that "Mount Fuji, Lake Shoji, and the hole are the holy trinity."

One day, a fisherman from Shoji Village died while out on his boat. The man's son went to visit Seigyo and said, "If these three really are the holy trinity, then bring my father back." Seigyo pondered the boys words and decided upon a course of action. He would discard his own life, taking on the pain of others and quietly departing this world with them. He stopped eating, and planned to commit *sokushinbutsu*, a process in which a monk enters mummification while still alive. This, they say, was the beginning of the Shoji no O-ana cult.

Many people claim that Aokigahara is full of "power spots." These are areas of natural beauty where, they claim, you can receive positive energy or spiritual power. As we've already discussed, Mount Fuji itself is considered to be the physical embodiment of a god, and people have long worshipped it. You can find numerous Asama or Sengen shrines around Mount Fuji where people worship both Konohanasakuya-hime and volcanoes in general. These shrines have been around for a long time, since at least before the eruption that created Aokigahara.

After the 864 eruption, views of Mount Fuji slowly began to change. No longer was it a mountain that people merely looked up to and revered, staying off its sacred slopes, but it slowly became a mountain that you could climb as well. Yamabushi, or mountain monks of the Shugendo religion—a mix of Shinto and Buddhism— frequently climbed Mount Fuji, and at the top they built Dainichiji Temple. Before long, any man, regardless of whether he was a monk or not, was permitted to climb the mountain. Women remained prohibited, but religious views towards the mountain were beginning to change.

Worship of Mount Fuji exploded during the Edo Period, and various ascetics and worshippers travelled from afar to visit. Mountain worship and religions have long had a foothold in Japan, and with Mount Fuji being the largest, it should come as no surprise that various shrines, temples, and cults sprang up around it. Much like Seigyo, the monk who found himself drawn to Mount Fuji, and one cave within Aokigahara in particular.

Located roughly in the centre of Aokigahara Forest you can find Kentoku Dojo, which, as explained earlier, was built by a lone monk sometime after Japan's defeat in World War II. The monk, a former soldier, planned to kill himself inside the forest. He wandered around Aokigahara for 10 years before he came upon the same cave that had called to the monk Seigyo; Shoji no O-ana. Whether it was fate or mere coincidence, the former soldier was moved to build a dojo where he could begin his own ascetic training. Locals helped him in his efforts, explaining that they "couldn't just let him die there."

It turned out that Seigyo was successful in his attempt at *sokushinbutsu*. He crawled deep into Shoji no O-ana and for 50 days sat in the darkness of the tiny, cramped cave, carrying out his religious training. After those 50 days had passed, he achieved self-mummification, and once people heard of this, they built a temple outside and erected a stone monument inside the cave to commemorate his sacrifice. Many old graves can be found in the area near the cave, although what happened to the original temple, nobody knows.

But what about the former World War II soldier turned monk? What did he hope to achieve with his training in the same location where Seigyo had succeeded in *sokushinbutsu*? To date, that still remains somewhat of a mystery. For a period, he did have believers who visited him while on pilgrimage to Mount Fuji, but reaching the dojo was difficult, and eventually these followers dried up.

Of those who spoke to the monk, all he revealed was that he was "working on a big project, and preparing for the coming of the gods." In his own words, "Japan is a special country! It is a country where millions of gods that control the skies reside." The monk claimed to have spoken to these gods, and they informed him that they did not create the planet Earth, which greatly surprised him. They had their own land, separate to Earth and free of humanity. Kentoku Dojo was a place where people could open their eyes to the coming of these gods, and when that day finally arrived, it would signal the end of humanity's time on Earth.

It was, in essence, a training ground to wait for the arrival of aliens who would wipe out humanity...

Needless to say, the monk of Kentoku Dojo worshipped something far different to Seigyo, and nobody has seen him for close to a decade now. Perhaps old age forced him out, or maybe he finally passed away after all these years. Nobody knows, but the building he erected to help "open people's eyes" now stands empty, a regular landmark and tour stop for people exploring Aokigahara's depths.

Aum Shinrikyo's Headquarters

There are numerous religious organisations that reside around Mount Fuji in this day and age. The list of these organisations goes on and on, many of them small in both size and number of followers, but one group that resided to the south of Aokigahara should ring a bell for most with an interest in Japanese news: Aum Shinrikyo, the cult responsible for the Tokyo subway sarin gas attacks.

Aum Shinrikyo set up headquarters in a village called Kamikuishiki. The "town" they established there was called Satian, meaning "truth." They finished construction of their first building there in April 1990, completing several more over the years until the area looked like a small town. It was there that Aum Shinrikyo stocked weapons and manufactured the poisonous sarin gas that killed so many in the 1995 Tokyo subway attack. When police raided the town, they found a stockpile of chemicals large enough to kill up to four million people, as well as other drug labs and safes full of US dollars. The cult's leader, Asahara Shoko, was also discovered in a secret room hidden inside one of the buildings.

The horrific acts that Aum Shinrikyo carried out over the years are covered in detail in numerous other books, but much of their preparations were carried out in Kamikuishiki, a stone's throw away from the main body of Aokigahara Forest. After the police raided their headquarters, the buildings were destroyed and levelled, and the area converted into a wide open park with a single memorial stone in the middle. The memorial stone commemorates all who suffered in the terrible acts Aum Shinrikyo carried out while stationed at the foot of one of Japan's holiest and most sacred sites: Mount Fuji, home of the god Konohanasakuya-hime.

FEATURES OF THE FOREST

AOKIGAHARA IS A UNIQUE FOREST. Starting from when Mount Fuji erupted in 864—destroying the previous forest that once existed there—to the stubborn trees that later attempted to take root in the hard lava bed, refusing to give up even when there was not enough soil to sustain their great heights, Aokigahara has witnessed a lot over the years. It has changed a great deal as well. Starting off as predominantly conifers, it has seen more deciduous trees growing in recent years.

People claim the topography of Aokigahara changes every 50 years as old trees grow too large to hold on and collapse, with new trees springing forth from their ruins. This constant shifting swallows old paths while newer ones develop. And as more people visit the forest, more things get discovered and more things get left behind. Aokigahara is constantly changing, but there are some things that remain steadfast. Let's take a look at some of the interesting features you can find inside.

15. HIDDEN TRASH AND TREASURES

A LOT OF things have been leftover in Aokigahara over the years. From rumours of illegal dumping, to its very long history as an important cultural and religious site, you can find all sorts of strange, mysterious, and sometimes downright wacky items hiding within its depths. Would you believe that there are ancient castle walls hidden deep within the trees? What about an abandoned jungle gym? The breadth and seemingly random nature of the things you can find inside Aokigahara might just surprise you. It's not just caves and corpses.

Statues

Just north of Fugaku Wind Cave you'll find several statues seemingly placed at random in the forest. One of those is a 40 centimetre high porcelain statue of Kannon, the goddess of mercy. People pray to Kannon to ease their suffering, and many miracles are attributed to her divine interference. A message is carved into the bottom half of the statue that states *"Inochi Taisetsu,"* meaning "life is precious." Her hands are held together in prayer, and the white of her porcelain makes her stand out amongst the rampant green of the forest. This statue has a tiny wooden roof to protect her from the rain, but she's presumably been in the forest for a long time, so her protection has rotted away over the years.

A few metres away from Kannon you can find a small porcelain statue of the Virgin Mary. Mary greatly resembles Kannon in size and appearance, meaning they likely came from the same hand. The Virgin Mary holds what appears to be baby Jesus in her arms and bears a similar message to Kannon. "*Inochi wo Taisetsu.*" Treat your life as a precious gift. Just like Kannon, she has a wooden rain roof, but the years have eaten away at it.

Both of these statues can be found not too far from the main path, and it's not hard to imagine why they were placed there. While nobody knows who left the statues, the "why" is clear enough from the carvings engraved in them. Your life is important. You should respect it. It doesn't matter what religion you follow, if you even follow one at all. Life is precious. Please reconsider your options.

Reports suggest that something may have happened to these statues in recent years. Visitors to Aokigahara have claimed difficulty in finding them, and others claim they've disappeared entirely. Perhaps the forest has finally grown up around them, or perhaps someone removed them. Like many other seemingly permanent fixtures of Aokigahara, it may be that they too may have moved on with the passing of time.

On the complete opposite side of the forest, you can find a tiny black cat statue a short distance from the highway. It appears to be somewhat melted and weathered, indicating that it's been there for quite some time. Again, nobody knows who made it or why it's been abandoned in the forest, but it's just another of the many strange items that people have left in Aokigahara for no good reason.

It's also not uncommon to stumble across tiny

armies of Jizo statues. Jizo straddles the line between this life and the afterlife, guiding children who have passed away before their parents safely to the other side, as well as helping lost travellers find their way. It should be no surprise then to find Jizo statues liberally placed within Aokigahara, perhaps by those hoping to guide lost souls on their way.

Pieces of bright rope lead from the walking paths to one statue in particular that has been affixed to a sturdy steel plate in the middle of the forest. Nearby is an abandoned shoe and other rubbish. It's possible that family members left it there to commemorate someone who took their life, hoping that Jizo would be able to guide them on their way.

Abandoned Charcoal Ovens

Not too far from the black cat statue in the west of Aokigahara is an infamous abandoned truck. The truck, a Toyota, has been there for quite some time and functions as a sort of landmark. Close to the truck, however, you'll find the remains of some ancient charcoal ovens built out of the hardened lava rock.

There are 10 in total, making a C shape and rising roughly a metre into the air. Surrounding these now abandoned ovens is a growth of white birch trees which can't be found anywhere else in Aokigahara. It's thought these trees were planted by the oven builders to use as fuel, and when the ovens were abandoned, the trees continued to grow freely. Many people tried to both live and work in Aokigahara during the Edo and Meiji periods, so these ovens have likely been leftover from those times.

Takeda Shingen's Stone Base

Mount Fuji erupted in 864. For a long time, the area that is now Aokigahara was unlivable, but by the late 1500s, the Takeda clan built Motosu Castle in what is now the western outreaches of the forest. There was, of course, no forest at the time—at least not as we know it today—and the castle was built to protect trade routes for the Takeda clan during the Warring States period.

Motosu Castle, named for nearby Lake Motosu, was built using the hardened lava rock bed, with the central area spanning roughly 50 by 15 metres. Over the years the castle fell out of use, and Aokigahara grew up around it. Now all that remains is a stone barrier referred to as "Takeda Shingen's Stone Base."

Roughly one to two metres high, and two metres long in a C shape, this stone base rises high like a barrier in the middle of the forest. When you remember that those stones were once the base for a massive castle, the forest becomes even more surreal.

Graffitied Tent

Within the danchi, roughly halfway between Fugaku Wind Cave and Narusawa Ice Cave, there once stood a lone blue tent. It's unclear when exactly it was left abandoned, but it's been there since at least the early 2000s. This particular tent became famous because the sides were spray painted in bright pink with various sayings. The most famous, *"mou ikite ikenai"*—which translates to "I can't live anymore"—was sprayed over the entrance. "Mama" was also sprayed in large letters on the side, and people discovered empty pill packets and burnt remains (rubbish, not human) inside. The tent was featured in a news special about Aokigahara on TV, and it also caught the attention of 2chan, the infamous anonymous Japanese online forums. After this, it became a famous landmark within the forest, although heavy snowfall eventually brought it down.

A nearby tree was also sprayed with the same paint, this time with *"norotte yaru."* I'll curse you. Sometime after 2003, this graffiti was changed by an unknown person or persons to *"iwatte yaru."* I'll celebrate you. The kanji for the initial word is very similar, and it only takes a small addition to one part of the character to completely change its meaning. This was likely done by a 2chan reader, but nobody knows for sure.

The tree has been there for so long that many people don't realise that the tree actually said *norotte yaru* to begin with. Posts on 2chan and Yahoo Questions often ask what exactly *"iwatte yaru"* is supposed to mean, and many answers assume that the original person simply mistook the kanji, not that it was changed after the fact. Tracing evidence back to the early 2000s reveals that it was indeed *norette yaru* first, however, and it wasn't changed until years later.

2chan

Speaking of 2chan and graffiti, travelling back towards Fugaku Wind Cave, and past the Kannon and Maria statues, you'll find a tree that's spray painted in red with the word *2chan*. 2chan has a fascination with all things dark and grotesque, so it's no surprise that the forums have an interest in Aokigahara as well. This was supposedly the work of 2chan's "spirit squad."

Around the same time, people discovered zippered yellow nylon bags hanging from trees around various areas of the forest. "*Jisatsu yamere!*" (Don't kill yourself!) was written on them in marker, beneath which it was signed "2ch Occult Forum @ Jukai." Beside the bags they found drinks and binoculars, and inside, notebooks and stationery. The notebooks appeared to chronicle a 2chan offline meet up inside the forest. It's unknown whether these were the same people who spray painted "2chan" on the tree, but it seems unlikely, as these folk went to the trouble of writing on plastic bags to hang from trees instead.

Altar Tree

Graffiti on trees is fairly common inside Aokigahara, as you can no doubt guess by now. Another tree of note inside the forest is the Altar Tree. This tree has the word "*shibou*" (death) spray painted on its side, beneath which several pieces of tiger rope hang like streamers from the tree's circumference. Numerous rocks have been placed at the tree's base as a makeshift altar, and offerings of drinks, flowers, and even yogurt have been left there. The tree was likely the site of a suicide, and family and friends created the altar in their memory. Bones were also reportedly found nearby, a possible oversight from the police who cleaned the area.

Suicide Note Tree

In the danchi, not too far west of the "I can't live anymore" tent, there's a tree that people have come to call the Suicide Note Tree. The following is carved into its trunk:

> *To whoever finds this, I'm terribly sorry.*
> *"I do this of my own free will."*
> *I return my body to my maker.*
> *This is nobody's fault.*
> *I'm sorry for harming this tree.*
> *I hope that it will grow strong and healthy.*
> *Please turn me into food for it.*
> *That is the only thing I can do right now.*

The note still stands to this day.

Jungle Gym

Of all the things you would expect to find inside Aokigahara, a jungle gym is probably not one of them. Yet, far to the south, you can find just that. Or at least, something that looks like one to the untrained eye...

The structure stands about 10 metres tall, made

of numerous criss-crossing metal pipes. That's roughly the size of a three to four story building. Considering its location, it seems even bigger than you might expect. So, what exactly is it, and how did it get there in the first place?

The structure is surrounded by a metal fence with a sign that says *"Danger. No Climbing."* Clearly someone didn't just dump a jungle gym in the middle of the forest, nor did they somehow manage to miraculously drag it there. It was built inside the forest for a purpose, and a fence erected to keep people out.

It turns out that the mystery "jungle gym" is a research outpost, and it's been there for close to 20 years. The pipes and signs have rusted over the years thanks to the harsh weather inside the forest, and the ground is littered with old water tanks. However, the jungle gym design once allowed scientists to reach high into the trees for their research, although it appears the structure is no longer in use. Now it sits abandoned, an enigma to all who happen upon it.

Honda Super Cub

Abandoned vehicles aren't an uncommon feature of large forests, and Aokigahara is no different. While the terrain may be difficult and unwieldy at best, the numerous walking paths the public use day in, day out are quite wide and convenient. Like the Toyota truck mentioned earlier, there are many abandoned vehicles inside the forest, and another of those is a Honda Super Cub motorcycle near Kentoku Dojo.

The handles were outfitted with extra gloves for protection against the cold, and two storage boxes sit on the back. Nobody knows what happened to the owner, or why the bike is all the way in the middle of the forest to begin with. Judging by its appearance, it's likely the owner travelled quite some distance, but for what purpose remains unknown.

An abandoned vehicle in one of the many car parks around the forest tends to tip off the police that someone has ventured into the forest to commit suicide, so perhaps the owner rode the bike inside hoping to avoid that. Perhaps they were exploring the forest and got lost, although this seems unlikely considering the bike's location. Whatever happened, the bike is now abandoned deep in the forest, waiting for nature to reclaim it.

16. ITEMS LEFT BEHIND

IN ADDITION TO the numerous oddities you can find inside Aokigahara Forest, such as abandoned vehicles and mysterious jungle gym-like structures, one more thing stands out, particularly for those who like to venture off the beaten track; personal items. When somebody enters the forest with no intention of leaving again, that means everything they bring with them will be left behind in the forest as well, and people leave a lot of strange and mundane things behind.

One interesting thing to note about the majority of bodies discovered in Aokigahara is the one thing they don't have on them; a wallet. Wallets are rarely found near or on corpses, and although you might be thinking, "Well, sure, because someone has taken it," that's generally not the case.

There are numerous reasons why people who are about to commit suicide leave their wallet behind. They don't want to be identified by their ID cards. They don't need the money. What are they going to do with a wallet after death? On the rare occasion a wallet is discovered by the body, it tends to be empty with nothing more than a few coins remaining, perhaps the change from their stop by the final convenience store on the way.

It's also not uncommon to find the burnt remains of a wallet for the same reasons; the person does not wish to be identified, and no longer has any use for their credit cards, money, or ID. Erasing those removes one's last links to the world, and once that is done, they can move on with the final step.

According to police, only approximately one in ten bodies discovered will have anything identifiable on them at all, let alone a wallet with ID.

As for what they do find, one particular trend noticed by police and volunteers is that the majority of women are discovered with large amounts of pills, strong alcohol (such as whisky), and important personal items on their body, while men tend to be found with rope, cigarettes, and one-cup sake (a popular and cheap brand of sake available at convenience stores).

One thing that seems to be shared across both genders is the appearance of the *Complete Manual of Suicide*. Even today it's not unusual to discover the book or its torn out pages beside a body, as well as the similarly named (but unrelated) *Complete Manual of Disappearance*. This particular book explains how to best disappear from society without anyone's help, working in tandem with the suicide manual.

Some people leave behind notebooks or suicide notes for those who find their bodies. One man, estimated to be in his 40s when he died, left behind a note that said, *"Shit, I'm getting sleepy, it's dark, it's so dark. Someone come get me. Help me."* Others have been found with portable CD players and stacks of CDs (the physical CD and DVD industry is still quite strong in Japan), and others with stacks of books and comics. More recently, it's not uncommon to find discarded cell phones and portable game players. One last thing to occupy the mind before the final act is committed.

One particularly bittersweet item that is

occasionally discovered is that of the *omamori*, a lucky charm or talisman obtained from shrines and temples meant to bring good luck and protection. Some people carry these right until the very end, even knowing they are about to end their own life. Omamori are often gifts from family members, so perhaps it's difficult to part from them in the final hour.

It's also not unusual to find discarded shoes, the likes of which you wouldn't imagine anyone could go so far into the forest wearing. Sandals, high heels, you name it. If someone doesn't have anything more suitable, it seems they won't let footwear stop them.

The forest is also littered with tents. Many people set up tents and spend the night in the forest, debating their decision. Some decide not to kill themselves and go home (leaving the tent behind). Others go through with it and also leave everything behind. Like the graffitied tent mentioned earlier, these are rarely pulled down by those who put them up, and it's up to others to clean them.

Aside from the personal items left behind by those who have committed suicide, you can also find all sorts of other trash and treasure inside the forest. Like a time capsule that has been dug up and spread throughout a dense, treacherous forest, people have found cans of drink (sometimes unopened) that were last sold in the late 80s, several decades later.

Unlike modern cans, where you pull the tab up and it presses the opening down, these cans were designed so that the pull tab itself came completely off, leaving a clean, open hole in the top of the can. These cans eventually fell out of favour because people were throwing the pull tabs on the ground and leaving rubbish everywhere, so they changed to the familiar cans we have now. People born after the 80s are unlikely to have ever seen these cans before, so coming across one in the depths of Aokigahara can be a surreal experience.

Many people enter Aokigahara to take photos and capture video. It's not strange to discover discarded or fallen lens caps, old film containers, compact cameras, and all sorts of other paraphernalia. Occasionally companies also film music videos and other promotional materials in the forest, but they're not the only ones. Numerous adult films have also been filmed inside the forest, presumably without the official approval required to do so, and people have reported one mattress in particular that has been left abandoned inside the forest for well over a decade now. Each year it degrades further and further. Apparently getting it in there was such a struggle that whoever took it in opted to leave it rather than try to drag it back out.

There have also long been rumours of companies illegally dumping rubbish in Aokigahara, but whether that's true or not, there *is* evidence that people have dumped their private rubbish in the forest. People have come across piles of old DVDs and video tapes, as well as worn out wallets and bags.

In the lead up to Mount Fuji being named as a UNESCO World Heritage Site in 2013, campaigns kicked into overdrive to keep Mount Fuji and its surrounding areas clean, and this meant the oft-neglected Aokigahara as well. The amount of rubbish cleaned up was astounding, and people often stumbled across such oddities.

17. TOURIST SPOTS

DESPITE ITS RENOWN as a suicide forest, Aokigahara is, first and foremost, a sightseeing spot. Long before *Nami no Tou* brought fame to the forest for all the wrong reasons, people visited Aokigahara to go sightseeing. In fact, millions of visitors each year still do. We've spoken about numerous tourist locations in this book already, but let's take a closer look.

Fugaku Wind Cave

Fugaku Wind Cave is one of two primary tourist attractions that people visit Aokigahara for; the other being Narusawa Ice Cave. Fugaku is technically a lava tube that formed in the east of Aokigahara when Mount Fuji erupted in 864. A lava tube forms when lava continues to flow beneath a hardened surface, and when the lava eventually stops and cools, a long cave is left behind. The cave is roughly 201 metres long and averages 8.7 metres in height, taking about 15 minutes to walk from one end to the other.

Fugaku gets its name from two things; one is *fuuketsu*, which is the Japanese word for wind cave. Fugaku is positioned such that air can circulate easily through it. The constant wind in and out of the cave can make it seem like it's breathing, a common feature of wind caves. The other is *Fugaku*, an alternative name for Mount Fuji. Combined, you literally have Mount Fuji Wind Cave.

The wind cave is so cold that icicles form even during the hot summer months. Around the time Aokigahara first formed, up until around 70 years ago, the cave was used to house silkworm eggs by the locals. Silkworm eggs appreciate cold temperatures, and the stable temperature all year round made the caves the perfect place to raise them. The average temperature is about 3 degrees Celcius, whether it's summer or winter outside.

Perhaps against expectations, the wind cave has no audible echo; the basalt walls absorb sounds, creating a unique cave experience. It's also home to a unique type of moss called "silicate hana." This moss appears bluish-white under light and seems to glow, making it a favourite for tourists of the cave. The official website states that Fugaku is suitable for both children and the elderly and costs just 350 yen per adult to enter.

The official store for Fugaku Wind Cave, *Mori no Eki Fuuketsu* (Forest Station Wind Cave), was renovated and reopened on April 26, 2011. There you can get local wines and specialities, hiking goods, other apparel you might need to safely pass through the cave, as well as tourist information. There's also a food corner to stock up on energy before your trek. This entrance is one of the most popular for entering Aokigahara in general, and often where cars are abandoned when people enter the forest with no intentions of leaving again.

Narusawa Ice Cave

Fugaku Wind Cave's companion, Narusawa Ice

Cave, is located roughly 700 metres to the southeast. Narusawa was declared a national monument in 1929 thanks to it being a "geological wonder." It formed during the 864 eruption by flowing around ancient parasitic volcanoes on Mount Fuji's side. This created a two-tunnel system that looks somewhat like a figure 8.

Like Fugaku, the average temperature in Narusawa Ice Cave is roughly 3 degrees all year round, and it is permanently covered in ice. Water constantly drips from the roof, creating the distinctive icicles that people associate with the cave. The cave was once used for refrigeration by the locals, and you can still find an old water pump inside. An ice wall towards the end of the cave reproduces how people used the cave for ice storage in the past by piling large blocks of ice on top of each other. If you go during the winter season, you may also be treated to the natural ice pillars that form, creating natural works of art before they thaw in the fall. And just like Fugaku, the cave was also used to keep silkworm eggs at a stable temperature all year long.

Narusawa Ice Cave is about 150 metres long and takes six to seven minutes to walk through. One tight section of the cave was formed when lava flowed over the massive trees that one stood in the area, forming a tree mold roughly 91 centimetres high. If you crouch, however, it's still possible to pass through it. It's somewhat sobering to realise you're walking through the place where a massive, ancient tree once stood, destroyed by a violent volcanic eruption. A helmet is highly recommended because the roof and walls are rather jagged and rough.

Inside the cave you can also find a hole labelled "*Jigoku Ana.*" Literally this means "Hell Hole," but in this case *jigoku* doesn't refer to hell. It refers to the fact that water disappears down the hole and nobody knows where it goes. A sign before it states:

Jigoku Ana
This hole is a pit. It is a dangerous hole where if you lose your footing, you'll never return again. According to legends, it goes all the way to a cave in Enoshima. Nobody knows just how far the hole goes.

Enoshima is an island just shy of 100 kilometres away from Mount Fuji, and the cave in question is Enoshima Iwaya Cave. Inside Iwaya Cave you'll find more about its supposed connection to Mount Fuji, confirming the old myth. There are two main sections of the cave, and although humans are unable to go past a certain point, the cave continues well past that point. How far? A sign states:

It's said that past this point connects all the way to Mount Fuji.

Needless to say, the story is just a myth. Narusawa Ice Cave was created when Mount Fuji erupted in 864. It formed out of hardened lava. Enoshima Iwaya Cave formed from waves washing away at a cliff-side over thousands of years. Both have sections of tunnels too small for people to enter, lending to the mystery that perhaps, just perhaps, somewhere they meet. Considering the circumstances of both their creations, however, that's highly unlikely. Makes for a great story though, and needless to say, the "Hole to Hell" is a popular sight for trembling tourists to take photos of.

Lake Sai Bat Cave

Although lesser known than its two brethren above, to the north of both you'll find Lake Sai Bat Cave. It may not house those seeking justice, but it is the largest of Aokigahara's three main caves. Lake Sai Bat Cave is 386.5 metres long, and like the other two, was also named a natural monument in 1929. If Fugaku is a wind cave because of its superior circulation, and Narusawa is an ice cave because it's constantly covered in ice, it's probably not hard to guess how Lake Sai Bat Cave got its name.

Lake Sai Bat Cave is home to over 500 bats. Bats reside in caves and caverns all throughout Aokigahara, but they are particularly concentrated here, and easily viewable to the public thanks to the large size of the cave. This cave was only opened to the public quite recently, in April 1998. Before that, land developments and trespassers threatened to drive the bats to extinction, so it was decided to run the cave officially as a tourist location to control the flow of people in and out of the area. A preservation deck was built towards the rear of the cave which has seen bat numbers rising in recent years, but it's good to keep in mind that a visit to the cave doesn't necessarily mean you will see any.

In addition to the mass of bats, Lake Sai Bat Cave's claim to fame is that, unlike its siblings, it's warm all year around. This is what draws so many bats there in the first place. The cave is also closed to the public from December 1 to March 19 each year to help preserve their living habitat.

Other than the tiny creatures of the night, you can also find lava stalactites and ropy-lava beds that formed when the lava that created the cave was exposed to the air. Certain parts of the cave are also narrow and claustrophobic, so it's not recommended for the elderly or those with mobility problems. You can borrow hard hats at the entrance to protect your head from the sharp, bumpy roof, but you'll still find yourself crouching for large parts of the walk, which can be uncomfortable at the best of times. The entire walk can take up to and around 30 minutes, making it somewhat lengthier than the other caves.

When you're done with Lake Sai Bat Cave, there's a museum outside where you can learn the history of the area, as well as spend your hard-earned cash on Bat Cave souvenirs. The museum itself is free, while entrance to the Bat Cave is 300 yen.

Dragon Cave

Did you know that you can find the Palace of the Dragon King inside Aokigahara? Legends have long said that a dragon resides in one of the caves inside the Sea of Trees. Not just any dragon, however, but Ryujin, father of Toyotama-hime, and one of the ancestors of the Japanese Imperial line. Ryujin presided over Senoumi before it was filled in by the 864 eruption, and even after this massive body of water was separated into smaller lakes, Ryujin hung around, taking one cave in particular as his home. That cave is *Ryuuguu Douketsu*, or the Dragon Cave.

Dragon Cave is roughly 60 metres long, and averages roughly 3 degrees Celsius all year around, just like Fugaku and Narusawa. In fact, it sits at roughly the midway point between those them and Lake Sai Bat Cave in the north. Long ago, travelling monks used to pray and train inside the cave on their way to Mount Fuji. Locals spoke of a white dragon that lived inside it, believed to be Ryujin himself. Even now, it's not uncommon for people to discover strange white lights that resemble a moving dragon when taking photos in the area.

In recent times, the cave has become too dangerous to enter alone, and approval must be sought from the government before entering. The rocks are unstable and there is fear of collapse. You can, however, visit a small shrine dedicated to Toyotama-hime at the mouth of the cave. Reaching the cave alone requires entry through a massive hole in the forest, so it's not hard to see how people over 1000 years ago assumed that it was the home of a dragon.

Although Senoumi may be no more, worship of Ryujin and Toyotama-hime never abated. Locals visited Dragon Cave during droughts to pray for rain and gather water from the icicles inside. This water literally saved their lives, and to this day the Ryujin Festival is celebrated each and every summer to give thanks to the goddess of water, Toyotama-hime.

It's interesting to note the parallels between the Palace of the Dragon King and Toyotama-hime with Urashima, an 8th century fairy tale. In the tale, a boy named Urashima Taro saves a turtle, who then allows him to ride on his back to the Palace of the Dragon King in thanks. A princess by the name of Otohime (Toyotama-hime) thanks Urashima Taro for his kindness in saving the turtle, and they spend several days together. Finally, the boy decides it's time to go home, and although she doesn't want him to leave, the princess relents, giving him a treasure box with a warning not to open it. When Urashima Taro gets home, he discovers that it hasn't been several days, but several years; close to 100, in fact. Everybody he ever knew is long gone. He opens the lid of the box and instantly turns into an old man.

This popular version is thought to be a variation of a much older tale which plays out much the same way, but instead of going to a Dragon Palace, the hero, Urashimako, goes with the princess to live in her world, a place of immortality. The word used for this is *furoufushi*, meaning no old age and no death. Perpetual youth. Immortality. Mount Fuji, as one of the sacred mountains of Japan, has often been associated with the word *fushi*—no death—as a play on its name. The Palace of the Dragon King and Toyotama-hime have long been associated with Mount Fuji, even in ancient folktales, so it's no surprise to find their home there.

If you wish to visit the Palace of the Dragon King yourself, or at least, the cave that's dedicated to him and his daughter, it's accessible from Highway 710. There's no parking, however, and you need to hike through the forest to reach it, so keep that in mind.

Oshino Hakkai

To the west of Aokigahara you'll find an area named Oshino Hakkai. While it may not be immediately recognisable in English, "*hakkai*" uses the Chinese characters for eight and sea. It's an area of eight ponds that were created in a different eruption that took place roughly 60 years before the one that created Aokigahara. Oshino, meanwhile, is the name of the village the ponds are in.

These ponds are amazingly clear and beautiful, full of fish and other marine life. They are another natural monument of Japan and feature as part of Japan's 100 best water features. Strictly speaking, however, they are not technically eight ponds. The ponds are all connected through tunnels beneath the hard lava surface and share in the same water source. It is only on the surface that they appear separate. You may remember the earlier story of the divers who tried to explore the tunnels to see where they went but got lost and died.

For many years, pilgrims on their way to Mount Fuji used to pass by Oshino Hakkai, visiting each of the ponds to pray and cleanse themselves in their clear waters. They were called the "spring of the gods." In 1843, the Eight Great Dragon Kings were each given a pond and worshipped as well. News of the ponds' beauty quickly spread, and Oshino Village itself saw a tourism boom as people came from all over to visit the sacred ground. You can make that same pilgrimage today and walk through a rather traditional-looking town with a stunning view of Mount Fuji in the background. It's easy to see why pilgrims and locals alike found the area to be a spiritual experience.

An ancient book discovered in Oshino Village by the name of *Miyashita Monjo* (Miyashita Archives) claimed that the area Oshina Hakkai stands on now was previously one giant lake by the name of Lake Utsu. Much like Senoumi was split into various lakes when Mount Fuji erupted in 864, Lake Utsu was split into Lake Yamanaka and Lake Oshino in the 802 eruption. Lake Oshino eventually drained and turned into a basin, but as the snow melted from Mount Fuji, the eight ponds sprang to life in its place. A survey was carried out to discover if this was true, but it was determined that Lake Utsu never existed, and this was merely a story passed down through the years. Regardless, Oshino Hakkai is rich in history, and well worth a stop if you're in the area.

Giant Cedar of Shoji

Just north of Lake Shoji, located inside the Suwa Shrine grounds, you'll find a massive Japanese cedar tree. It is popularly known as the Giant Cedar of Shoji, or the Thousand Year Cedar. This massive tree stands at 40 metres tall, with its roots spreading out over 12 metres in circumference underground. Like the name states, this tree is believed to be over 1000 years old. 1200 years, to be more precise. Meaning that the tree was likely one of the first to grow back after the numerous eruptions of Mount Fuji in the 800s.

The area it stands on was once a highway linking Kai Province (modern day Yamanashi Prefecture) with Suruga Province (modern day Shizuoka Prefecture). Takeda Shingen's castle was built just south of this highway, in what is now Aokigahara Forest, during the Warring States period to watch the flow of traffic coming in and out of the all-important area.

This tree was already old when Takeda Shingen himself passed by. It's positively ancient now, and it's also worshipped as such. The tree is a *goshinboku*, or sacred tree. It is so old and important that a spirit now resides within it. This one tree has seen the coming and going of over 1200 years of historical changes, survived over 1200 years of fierce weather and natural disasters, and withstood over 1200 years of internal and external war. But it almost wasn't to be.

In 1966, a typhoon nearly destroyed the tree, burying it beneath an avalanche of rocks and soil. Yet this was still not enough to bring it down, and the sacred tree was dug out and restored to its former glory.

The tree is, of course, free to visit, and has proven itself sturdier than the entirety of Aokigahara itself.

Iyashinosato Ancient Japanese Village

A few hundred metres from Lake Saiko you'll find Iyashinosato, a reconstructed ancient Japanese village. This village on the edge of Aokigahara Forest was once a real village left abandoned after it was destroyed by a terrible typhoon in 1966 (the same typhoon that buried the Giant Cedar of Shoji). 94 villagers died, and those who remained moved to the opposing shore of Lake Saiko, leaving the devastated remains of their former village behind.

Many years later, it was decided to restore the village and use it as an open-air museum, rather than leaving the land to languish forever doing nothing, and in 2006, Iyashinosato opened. The traditional thatched huts now sell souvenirs, double as restaurants, and display traditional arts and crafts. You can also find a museum dedicated to the disaster that destroyed the village, as well as dress up in traditional kimono for a more authentic experience.

It costs 350 yen to enter, and it's open all year around.

Aokigahara Hiking Course

If you're looking for a slightly more structured walk through Aokigahara, and somewhere away from the main tourist thoroughfare of Fugaku Wind Cave and Narusawa Ice Cave, you can take part in the Aokigahara Hiking Course. This is a walk through Aokigahara itself and visits several points of interest.

Starting from Lake Saiko Bat Cave, you'll see various flora and fauna along the way, as well as interesting caves and trees that are marked with signs explaining what they are. The walk continues to Lake Saiko Wild Bird Forest Park, home to over 60 different types of birds, and then up to Iyashinosato. From there you can take the bus back to Lake Saiko Bat Cave, or continue exploring the area.

There's plenty to see and do in and around Aokigahara, and if you enjoy exploring nature, you'll find more than enough to keep you occupied.

18. SEASONAL CHANGES

DEPENDING ON THE time of year you visit Aokigahara, the forest will look and feel different. The forest fully experiences all four seasons, and the time of year you visit will determine what you'll be able to see and do. Here's how the Sea of Trees changes throughout the year.

Spring

Spring marks the start of the new school and business year in Japan. It's the season of cherry blossoms, flower viewings, and new beginnings. Aokigahara is no different, and after its harsh winter, spring sees it blooming back to life.

Yamanashi Prefecture is usually not too cold at this time of year, but Aokigahara sits 1000 metres above sea level, so it can still be somewhat chilly. Even if you don't plan to visit any of the caves, it's still a good idea to carry a jacket, just in case. If the previous winter has seen heavy snowfall, there might still be snow lingering on the ground in April.

Spring also reportedly sees a marked rise in the number of dead bodies discovered in the forest. Fewer tourists venture off the track during the cold autumn and winter seasons, meaning those who commit suicide during this time are less likely to be found.

According to Aokigahara regulars, Christmas and New Year's tend to see a spike in suicides, as well as early spring thanks to the "May blues." *Gogatsu Byou*, as it's known in Japanese, is a phenomenon where people find themselves unable to cope with the changes and pressures of a new school or job. It's not uncommon for people to fall into a depression during this time, which some may struggle to get out of. This increased activity in the forest thus means that more bodies tend to be found.

The Shibasakura Festival also takes place in spring just across the road from Aokigahara, which brings in so many tourists from all around the country that there are often traffic jams lasting for hours. It's also not uncommon to come across the Japanese defence forces training in the forest whilst hiking during early spring; the rough terrain no doubt makes for a great natural training ground. And while the forest is made up of mostly evergreen trees, you might still come upon some fresh green growth as the season changes, so keep an eye out.

Summer

Summers are hot in the Sea of Trees. You won't find a lot of bugs inside Aokigahara like you might elsewhere, but there's still a decent amount of mosquitoes and spiders. You can expect to work up a sweat while exploring the hiking trails, but it's recommended that you wear long sleeves, regardless. Chances are high bugs will try to bite you, or you might trip and scratch yourself on one of the many pointy branches and roots in the forest. It's also a good idea to keep some bug spray on you at all times.

After the cold of winter has gone and spring has

seen nature blooming back to life, summer is a lively season in the Sea of Trees. You can find numerous mushrooms and tiny plants growing wild and free, as well as all sorts of pine cones on the hiking courses. Summer is also the prime season for camping, with many camp grounds surrounding the nearby lakes, although you may occasionally stumble across someone camping inside the forest as well.

Mount Fuji's climbing season begins in July, which sees another rush of tourists to the area. Many people choose to travel through Aokigahara on their way to the sacred mountain, just like the pilgrims of old. The foot of the mountain becomes lively once more, and you'll come across all sorts of people hiking the trails. This is Aokigahara's busiest season.

Autumn

While the rest of the country is still hot, Aokigahara starts to cool down, making this a great season for hiking as well. If you're not a fan of big crowds and sweating your body weight just by walking, autumn is a great time to experience all Aokigahara has to offer.

Again, while the majority of Aokigahara is made up of evergreen trees, you can still find a healthy amount of trees that begin changing colour during autumn. As with cherry blossom viewing in spring, watching the changing leaves in autumn is another popular pastime in Japan, and the area near Fugaku Wind Cave is particularly beautiful.

Enjoy a peaceful walk through the forest and take in all nature has to offer, and if you want a real nice view, drop by Koyodai Observatory to catch a glimpse of Aokigahara spread out as far as the eye can see; red, yellow, and green trees alike.

Winter

There's a common misconception that you're not allowed to walk around Aokigahara during winter, but that's not true. The forest is never officially closed to the public, and even during winter you're free to explore. Of course, winter in the forest is cold, and the snow often doesn't make for the best hiking conditions, meaning that the area naturally sees a drop in tourists and regulars alike.

Winter sees the return of icicles in Aokigahara's caves, and some of them remain open all year around. Fugaku Wind Cave, for example, is open all year, and the temperature inside remains constant. While it might seem freezing in summer, during winter it can seem a nice change of pace to the freezing temperatures outside. If you're lucky, you might even see a hibernating bat or two.

You can also visit the nearby Saiko Wild Bird Forest Park for their annual frost-covered tree festival. This takes place around the end of January and start of February. Here you can view the massive trees covered entirely in ice, as well as enjoy light shows and art displays.

December through to February is the peak snow season for Aokigahara, and while it doesn't tend to pile high, it can be enough to make walking through the forest quite difficult. Chances of slipping on the wet ice rise, making it even more dangerous than usual. If you're a budding cameraman, however, this is a great time of year to capture some unique photos of the forest. Just make sure that you're dressed appropriately for the cold, and keep in mind that the freezing conditions may affect your batteries, so have a backup plan in case they die.

AFTERWORD

FROM ITS BEGINNINGS AS A single seed dropped on a hardened lava bed, to its time as a site of worship, and its modern infamy as a suicide spot, Aokigahara has been through lifetimes of changes. Against all odds it sprang to life, spreading so far and wide that it came to be called the "Sea of Trees" despite the near-barren rock it sits on. Numerous generations have tried to tame the forest, and all have failed. It thrives where no forest should, and despite its reputation as dark and terrifying, it remains one of the most popular tourist destinations in Japan. It's breathtaking, it's resilient, and it's unique. It's not just a "suicide forest," and although it's a struggle, efforts are underway to change the public's perception.

Aokigahara is a stunning virgin forest with a long and fascinating history. There truly is no other place like it.

SOURCES

The following sources were consulted whilst researching for this book:

Hayano, Azusa. *Aokigahara Jukai wo Kagaku Suru.* Tokyo: Hihyosya, 2006.

Kurihara, Toru. *Jukai no Arukikata.* Tokyo: East Press, 2005.

Murata, Ramu. *Jukai Ko.* Tokyo: Shobunsha, 2018.

The following web pages were also accessed before August 2019 for research:

5 Channel. "Shichirin de 3sai no Nijo to Murishinjuu."
https://news19.5ch.net/test/read.cgi/newsplus/1100681734/

Asahi. "Jisatsu no Meisho."
http://www.asahi.com/special/08016/OSK200902280056.html

Asahi. "Shichi Nenburi 'Maboroshi no Mizuumi'."
http://www.asahi.com/travel/aviation/TKY201110050547.html

Asyura. "Aokigahara Jukai de Shakkinku no Oyako Murishinjuu."
http://www.asyura2.com/0403/nihon12/msg/301.html

Excite News. "Hae no Tamago no Namida wo Nagasu Itai mo…!"
https://www.excite.co.jp/news/article/Tocana_201808_post_17623/

Excite News. "(Kouhen) Aokigahara Jukai ni Sumu Itanshatachi wo Mita!"
https://www.excite.co.jp/news/article/Bucchinews_989/?p=2

Filmarks. "JUKAI." https://filmarks.com/movies/63716/no_spoiler

Fujigoko.TV. "Yuushi no Fujisan." http://www.fujigoko.tv/mtfuji/vol1/fjhis03.html

Fujisan NET. "Shizuka de Utsukushii Mori Torimodosu." https://www.fujisan-net.jp/RENSAI/021_04.html

Fujiyama Navi. "Oshino Hakkai." https://www.fujiyama-navi.jp/entries/jAlqO

Global Times. "Man Living Near Japan's 'Suicide Forest' Hopes Music." http://www.globaltimes.cn/content/1133226.shtml

J-Cast News. "Imadani Jisatsusha Kyuuin Suru." https://www.j-cast.com/2008/03/09017443.html?p=all

My Game News Flash. "Jisatsu no Meisho." http://jin115.com/archives/52004362.html

Official Travel Guide Yamanashi. "Lake Sai Bat Cave." https://www.yamanashi-kankou.jp/foreign/english/spot/056.html

Oshino Village Sightseeing Association. "Oshino Hakkai." http://www.oshino.jp/spot_8lakes.php

Shinbun Akahata. "Shakkin Jisatsu Mizugiwa de Fusegu." https://www.jcp.or.jp/akahata/aik07/2007-07-25/2007072515_02_0.html

So Tai-ki. "Journal d'Ohaka." http://www.eonet.ne.jp/~so-tai-ki/journal2001.7.htm

Subarashiki Nihon no Keshikitachi. "Ryuugyuujou wa Sonzai Shita!?" https://www.narisuba.com/entry/2017/10/19/224026

Toyokeizai Online. "Fuji no Jukai ni Tsutawaru 'Itsusu no Toshi Densetsu' no Shinjitsu." https://toyokeizai.net/articles/-/231647

Tripnote. "Jitsu wa Ki ni Naru! Aokigahara Jukai tte Konna Toko!" https://tripnote.jp/yamanashi/aokigahara-jukai

Wind Cave & Ice Cave. "Fugaku Fuketsu Wind

Cave." https://www.mtfuji-cave.com/en/wind_cave/

Yamanashi. "Aokigahara Jukai Sansaku Course."
https://www.yamanashi-kankou.jp/kokuritsukoen/jp/miryoku/hiking/course3.html

Yamanashi Prefecture. "Fuji/Toubu Hokensho ni Okeru Jisatsu Boushi no Torikumi ni Tsuite." https://www.pref.yamanashi.jp/ft-hokenf/suicide-guideline1.html

WANT EVEN MORE JAPANESE HORROR?

Read a sample from *Toshiden: Exploring Japanese Urban Legends*, also by Tara A. Devlin.

Sugisawa Village

Hidden deep within the mountains of Aomori Prefecture there exists a village called Sugisawa. One day a man from the village went crazy. Within a single day he killed everyone living in the village and then took his own life.

Nobody knows why he went crazy, nor why he went on such a violent crime spree. But the end result of this horrific crime remained the same: Sugisawa Village became empty.

The events of that day were so cruel that the local government decided to leave the village abandoned, and at the same time deny anything ever took place. They then erased all trace of the village from the local maps.

Luckily the village was deep in the mountains, so it was easy to cover the events up. But, of course, they couldn't erase the fact that the horrific crime *did* take place in the first place.

There were rumours of thick bloodstains all over the village, and those who approached the village would undoubtedly be cursed by the evil spirits that lived there.

Furthermore, according to the legend, it's impossible to reach Sugisawa unless you leave the straight path that leads further into the mountains. Then you will find a sign with a warning standing at the entrance. That sign states, "You may enter, but do so at your own risk."

You can also find an old red shrine gate at the entrance, and a stone shaped like a skull sitting at its feet.

ABOUT

The legend of Sugisawa Village first appeared in the 1990s, although the events mentioned in the legend itself are purported to take place early in the Showa era (the late 1920s and early 30s). The story was one of the first and biggest to be spread through the internet in a time when it was just starting to take off. The story became so popular that several media outlets picked up on it, and it was through the TV show *Kiseki Taiken Unbelievable* in 2000 that it truly reached the masses. The episode set out to find this fabled village and determine whether it actually existed or not. They searched throughout not just Aomori Prefecture but similar stories all over Japan, but in the end they never found it. The program then claimed that Sugisawa Village must exist in a space-time warp, able to appear and disappear at will. After the program aired many people set out to find the village themselves, uploading blog entries and later YouTube videos on their findings, many of which you can still watch on the internet today. Despite claims to the contrary, nobody has ever found the 'real' Sugisawa Village of legend, and it's unlikely anyone ever will.

HISTORY

The legend of Sugisawa Village began in Aomori, the place the village is supposed to be located. There was a real village call Kosugi. It was a small village in the Obatakezawa district of Aomori City. This area received its name because of "a mountain stream that flows through the cedar forest." *Sugi* means cedar and *sawa* means marsh or mountain stream. People would say they were going to 'the cedar,' which sounded a lot like the word 'Sugisawa' in Japanese, and thus it came to be affectionately called that. However, the village was only accessible by foot, and as the years passed it became abandoned because of depopulation, not a murderous crime spree. So how did the benign village of Sugisawa become the fabled site of such a horrific crime?

There was an actual crime in 1938, the same time the Sugisawa legend is supposed to have happened, that took place in the small village of Kamo, close to Tsuyama in Okayama Prefecture. A man, Mutsuo Toi (21 at the time) killed 30 people and injured three before killing himself. Toi had tuberculosis, and in his suicide note claimed that the villagers treated him cruelly, so he wished to extract revenge. He snuck into people's homes over the course of a single night and using a shotgun, katana and axe killed over half the village's occupants, before killing himself at dawn. Although Okayama and Aomori are separated by quite a distance, somehow the story of this crime in Okayama was adapted to the abandoned village in Aomori and became the modern day legend of Sugisawa Village.

There exist even more crazy rumours about the truth of Sugisawa. Some claim it's actually a cover-up for a secret government Echelon base, while others have claimed it's a settlement for old Templar Knights. Apparently you can find Jesus Christ's grave in Aomori Prefecture as well. Who knew?

FINDING THE VILLAGE

There are several key signs that you have stumbled upon Sugisawa Village:

- There is a sign at the entrance that states, "You must not proceed past this point. There can be no guarantee for your life if you do." There are variations on the exact wording, but in every version the sign states that if you go past it, you will be in big trouble.
- There is an old, red shrine gate at the entrance to the village, beneath which you'll find a stone that's shaped like a skull.
- Upon entering the village you'll find several abandoned buildings with bloodstains on the walls.

WITNESS'S ACCOUNTS

There are several creepypastas on the internet from people who claim to have visited Sugisawa. The following is a common tale shared amongst friends of friends:

One day, two young men and a woman went for a drive deep in the mountains when they got lost and stumbled upon an old, beat up shrine gate. Beneath the gate there were two large stones, one of them shaped like a skull.

The young driver saw it and remembered a rumour he'd heard long ago. The rumour was that a skull found at the bottom of a shrine gate was a sign of the entrance to Sugisawa.

The two men got out of the car; however, the young woman said to them, "I'm scared, let's get out of here." They decided to search the village, however, and all went in together.

About 100 metres after passing under the shrine gate they suddenly found a large open area before them with four old, abandoned buildings. The three of them stepped inside one of the buildings and inside they found a large amount of dried blood on the walls.

The two men felt a shiver run up their spines, and the woman suddenly cried out.

"Hey, there's something strange about this place. I can feel a presence!"

The three of them fled the building in surprise, and as they did, they felt like they were being surrounded by a large number of people.

The three of them ran for the car. However, something was wrong. No matter how much they ran they couldn't seem to reach the car.

The open space to the car should have only been 100 metres, and it was a straight path so there's no way they could have gotten lost. Even so, as the three of them kept running and running they couldn't escape from Sugisawa.

Unawares, the woman suddenly found herself separated from the two men, and as she kept running for what felt like forever she somehow finally found herself back at the car. Thankfully, the keys were still in the ignition. She climbed into the driver's seat to go and get help and turned the key to start the car.

However, no matter how much she turned the key the car refused to start. On the verge of tears she kept turning the key, over and over, trying to get the car to go.

Then...

Don don don.

A large sound suddenly reverberated from the windscreen. She looked and noticed the windscreen was covered in bloody red handprints.

No, not just the windscreen. Countless bloody red handprints appeared on all the windows as though they were all being beat upon at the same time.

The woman crouched down in fear, and before long she fainted...

The next morning one of the locals, out for a morning walk, stumbled upon the bloody car and the dumbfounded young woman inside. Her hair had turned white from fear overnight.

She was taken to the hospital where she explained her terrifying experience. Afterwards she disappeared and was never seen again. Her two male friends were also never found.

The following is a tale from someone calling themselves Matsu-san:

This is a story someone who went to Sugisawa Village told me. They were driving up the mountain when they finally found a gravel road they could pass through when they found a sign. They ignored it and kept going before they realised they'd arrived at Sugisawa Village. The place apparently stank of garbage.

There were a few wooden buildings and a lot of rubbish lying around. This person felt someone watching them, though, and feeling creeped out they left. A few days later a friend who was with the person at the time died.

And the following is from Keiko-san in Saitama:

I went to Aomori Prefecture to go mountain climbing. About two hours into climbing the area was wrapped in fog, and I couldn't see well. I made my way slowly up the mountain so I didn't fall and there were several villages along the way.

Then it was like there was this village smack bang in the middle of the jungle. It was dark, so I pulled out my torch and approached it. There were six buildings in total, and I went from house to house checking each one. There was no sign that anybody lived there. All I saw were two cats.

While I was walking around, I sensed somebody approaching me, yet when I looked around nobody was there. It was incredibly strange.

There were houses further back in the village as

well, but I was too scared to go and look at them. About 20 minutes later I noticed a man standing behind me. He was wearing a straw hat and had pale skin and blue eyes. I said hello, but he said nothing in reply. I paid him no attention and kept walking, but then he suddenly screamed and ran at me.

I ran and finally reached the sign that stated I was back on the mountain climbing track. That was the first time I'd ever been so scared. I still don't know what that guy was doing there now. I told people about what happened there, but nobody believes me.

The following message was posted by someone claiming to be a police officer in Aomori:

Sugisawa Village exists. It's close to Aomori Airport...
But you must never go looking for it, and please don't enter it half-cocked.
Because if you do, you'll never come back...

MEDIA

There have been several documentaries and even a movie made about Sugisawa Village over the years. It's featured in several manga, multiple TV shows, and you can even play a game on your mobile phone where you try to escape from the village. You can find a full list of all these at the Japanese Wikipedia site..

WANT EVEN MORE?

Also available in *Toshiden: Exploring Japanese Urban Legends*
Volume One
Volume Two

Reikan: The most haunted locations in Japan

The Torihada Files:
Kage
Jukai
Kirei

Kowabana: 'True' Japanese scary stories from around the internet:
Volume One
Volume Two
Volume Three
Origins
Volume Five

Read new stories each week at Kowabana.net, or get them delivered straight to your ear-buds with the *Kowabana* podcast!

ABOUT THE AUTHOR

Tara A. Devlin studied Japanese at the University of Queensland before moving to Japan in 2005. She lived in Matsue, the birthplace of Japanese ghost stories, for 10 years, where her love for Japanese horror really grew. And with Izumo, the birthplace of Japanese mythology, just a stone's throw away, she was never too far from the mysterious. You can find her collection of horror and fantasy writings at taraadevlin.com and translations of Japanese horror at kowabana.net.

Printed in Great Britain
by Amazon

20544600R00089